What in the World is a Christian?

What in the World is a Christian?

by John Blanchard

COVERDALE
EASTBOURNE

© John Blanchard 1975
First published 1975
First reprint 1977

ISBN 0 902088 78 5

By the same author

NOT HEARERS ONLY (4 vols.)
RIGHT WITH GOD
LIVING AND LEARNING THE CHRISTIAN LIFE
READ MARK LEARN

Printed in Great Britain for Kingsway Publications Ltd.,
Lottbridge Drove, Eastbourne, East Sussex BN23 6NT
by Hunt Barnard Printing Ltd., Aylesbury, Bucks.

To PETER, ERIC, DAVE and DEREK

in gratitude for years of holy and
hilarious fellowship

CONTENTS

INTRODUCTION

'Who *are* you?'

The park-keeper's question cracked like a rifle shot across Frankfurt's Tiergarten, jolting back to some kind of reality the ragged figure slouched untidily on a bench. Slowly he raised his head, looked sadly at the official and said 'I wish to God I knew!'

Arthur Schopenhauer, one of his country's greatest philosophers, had spent years wrestling with the problems of the universe and of man's existence on the earth - but he had no clear picture of his own identity. The whole of his life was impoverished as a result.

Many Christians are spiritually impoverished for a similar reason – failure to understand and appreciate their own spiritual identity. This may be because of a lack of sound teaching, or their own superficial approach to the Scriptures, or a restless chasing after mystical 'experience' or 'thrills' which leave them blown out without being built up. Whatever the reason, the result is always sub-normal Christianity.

I have long been convinced that there is no substitute for straightforward Biblical teaching in order to produce healthy, balanced and progressive Christians. Doctrine has a built-in dynamic to be found nowhere else. As Jesus put it, 'The truth will make you free' (John 8.32). Basic Biblical truth, simply understood and applied, sets the Christian free – from errors, excesses and eccentricities. Whether the issue is one of doctrine or practice, theology or morality, public worship or private living, the Christian's starting-point should always be 'What does the Scripture say?' (Romans 4.3)

9

To look at the problem from another angle, too many Christians are suffering from homiletical shell-shock. They have been blasted and blistered, urged, exhorted and challenged (perhaps the most over-used word in Christendom) by one preacher after another to improve their spiritual standard of living, but often without a Biblical explanation of what a Christian *already is*. Yet surely this is the only place to begin? To put it in a nutshell, the Bible's moral teaching amounts to this – *we are to become what we are!* It is my conviction that if all Christians, and especially those young in the faith, could grasp this, their lives would be wonderfully enriched – and it is this conviction that led to the series of studies contained in this little book.

If you are looking for a detailed and scholarly exposition of Scripture, profound in depth and prophetic in element, then you have the wrong book! My aim has merely been to examine in a simple and straightforward way some of the phrases the Bible uses to describe a Christian, and to apply the truth to everyday Christian living.

The outline of the series first took shape when I was flying between Dallas and Miami, towards the end of a preaching tour in America, and the material in its original form was taught during Bible Hours on summer house parties held under the auspices of The Movement for World Evangelization, notably at Les Avants-sur-Montreux, Switzerland. I am grateful to MWE for giving me the privilege of leading those very happy occasions.

As with previous books, Sheila Hellberg has done a superb job of typing and re-typing the manuscripts, and I am also greatly indebted to my good friend Paul Hill who suggested numerous improvements at the final drafting stage.

If this book helps you be a wiser and better Christian, their efforts and mine will have been more than amply rewarded.

Croydon,
Surrey.   JOHN BLANCHARD

Chapter 1

A Son

With all due deference to storks and gooseberry bushes, we can state as a categorical fact that life begins with birth! And when all the pseudo-Christian theories have been examined and rejected, we can state equally firmly that spiritual life begins with spiritual birth. Unless a person has experienced the new birth, he has not even begun the Christian life. As Jesus said plainly to Nicodemus, 'Truly, truly, I say to you, unless one is born anew, he cannot see the kingdom of God' (John 3.3). A man does not become a Christian as a result of his upbringing, his moral effort, his religious affiliation, nor in any other way except by an experience so radical that Jesus called it being 'born anew'. This explains why the Bible repeatedly describes a Christian as a son (or child) of God. Old Testament believers are described as 'Sons of the living God' (Hosea 1.10). The Apostle Paul tells the Christians at Rome that 'All who are led by the Spirit of God are the sons of God' (Romans 8.14), and he encourages those at Philippi to be 'blameless and innocent, children of God without blemish in the midst of a crooked and perverse generation' (Phil. 2.15). He writes to the Christians at Galatia and reminds them that 'in Christ Jesus you are all sons of God, through faith' (Galatians 3.26). The Apostle John writes 'See what love the Father has given us, that we should be called children of God; *and so we are* . . . . 'Beloved, we are God's children *now*' (1 John 3.1–2).

What a wonderful truth this is! Christians are not merely people who are trying to be God's followers. They are members of his family, and have the right to claim that

11

astonishing relationship with the eternal God. Notice that I said the *right* to claim it. Let me show you that from the Bible. In the opening chapter of John's Gospel we read that Jesus 'came to his own home, and his own people received him not'. Then, in the next verse, John says 'But to all who received him, who believed in his name, he gave power to become children of God . . .' (John 1.12). To understand what John is really saying here we have to grasp the meaning of the word translated 'power' in many of our English versions of the Bible. There are six different Greek words translated by the English word 'power'. The one most commonly used is the word *dunamis*, from which we get the word 'dynamite', and it obviously means force, or strength, or might. But that is not the word John uses here. The word here is *exousia*, which means 'right' or 'authority'. To illustrate its meaning, let us take a look at some other verses where this word is used, before coming back to this amazing statement by John. Speaking to the Jews at Jerusalem, Jesus said 'For as the Father has life in himself, so he has granted the Son also to have life in himself, and has given him *authority* to execute judgment, because he is the Son of Man' (John 5.27). Jesus was not saying that he had the strength to pass judgment on men, overwhelming them by some supernatural force, but that he had the right to do so. It was part of his office as the Son of Man. Later, speaking about his own earthly human life, he said 'No one takes it from me, but I lay it down of my own accord. I have *power* to lay it down, and I have *power* to take it again; this charge I have received from my Father' (John 10.18). Now of course we could say that it required divine dynamite (dunamis) to raise Jesus from the dead – but again that is not the point that Jesus is making here. What he is saying is that he had the *authority* to do this: authority to lay his life down and authority to come to life again. As God, he acted with divine power: as man, he acted with divine authority, and this is the point to remember at this moment.

Then, in a wonderful prayer in John 17, Jesus reminds his heavenly Father that he had given him '*power* over all flesh, to give eternal life to all whom thou hast given him' (John

17.2). Again, Jesus is not speaking about some kind of spiritual brute force. He is speaking about *authority*, about a divine right to rule in the affairs of men. That is what Jesus had been given. Nobody could deny it, nobody could dispute it, nobody could deprive him of it. It was his by divine right.

This, then, is the word we have in John 1.12, where we are told that those who receive Christ, and who believe in his name, are given *'power* (the authority, the right) to become children of God'. John is not saying that God gives us power to become children of God by ourselves, but rather that he has made us children of God by his own power, and gives us the authority to say that he has done so! Do you see the difference? And *every* Christian has been given that authority! Young or old, weak or strong, obedient or disobedient, every Christian is a child of God, and has been given divine authority to make that claim. What a tragedy that so many Christians seem to be lacking that happy, positive assurance. Some seem to have no more than the courage of their confusions on the matter, while Billy Graham once said 'Many Christians have settled down under their doubts as though they had contracted an incurable disease'. When a Christian is in that state, his witness loses its cutting edge, the glow and warmth goes out of his worship, and he knows little or nothing of what Paul calls 'joy and peace in believing' (Romans 15.13). For many people who are in that unhappy state, I believe that the road to recovery begins by grasping the wonderful truth that, whatever their doubts and fears, the fact remains that God has given them the status of being children of God, members of his family, objects of his special and eternal love and care.

Having established that one basic fact, we can move on to look at three aspects of this great truth. The first two are doctrinal, and form the real heart of this study, while the third is practical, and points to the application of this truth in the Christian's life.

1. *THE MYSTERY OF BEING A SON OF GOD.*

Let us go back for a moment to the confrontation between Jesus and Nicodemus in John 3. After the religious leader's opening comment, Jesus replied 'Truly, Truly, I say to you, unless one is born anew he cannot see the kingdom of God'. Apparently stunned by this amazing answer, Nicodemus asked 'How can a man be born when he is old? Can he enter a second time into his mother's womb and be born?' (John 3.4). Without going any further, it is obvious that Nicodemus had already missed the point. He was miles away from what Jesus was saying. In fact the only other recorded words of Nicodemus in the whole dialogue formed another question, when in reply to what Jesus told him about the work of the Holy Spirit, he asked 'How can this be?' (v. 9). Nicodemus had problems! He could not grasp the difference between a new start and a new life. He could not understand the need for a spiritual birth as well as a physical one. Jesus called him 'a teacher of Israel' (v. 9) – but on this issue he was back in the kindergarten! Now of course, as Christians, we can look back at this incident and claim to know more than Nicodemus. We can pronounce on his ignorance. It is perfectly obvious to us that Jesus was speaking of a spiritual and not a physical birth. That is no mystery to us. That may be so, but there is something that needs to be very carefully underlined in our minds. However much we can now understand of what Jesus meant when he spoke to Nicodemus, let us never for one moment forget that the new birth *is* a mystery. There are things about it that we can never understand. Some forms of evangelism today seem to me to run the risk of evacuating all the mystery from the new birth and reducing it to a formula, a technique, a routine, or a procedure. You just stand up, walk out, sign on, and you are in. But that is a tragedy and a travesty. Take away the mystery from the new birth and you have taken away its majesty. It *is* a mystery, and I want us to take note of just two aspects of it that we can never fully understand.

14

Firstly, its operation is mysterious.

Notice what Jesus said to Nicodemus -- 'The wind blows where it wills, and you hear the sound of it, but you do not know whence it comes or whither it goes; so it is with every one who is born of the Spirit' (v. 8). This picture of the wind came across very dramatically to me one day while I was preaching at a convention in Texas. It was a perfect June day, with a clear blue sky, not a breath of wind, and the temperature in the upper 80's. A colleague and I had a swim at our motel, relaxed in the sun for a while, and then, towards the end of the afternoon, made our way to our room to change for the evening rally. As we reached our room, the curtain flickered gently in a sudden gust of wind. A moment or so later it did so again, more strongly this time. Within five minutes the sky began to cloud over, and just moments later we were in the middle of a howling gale. Garden furniture was being flung about like matchwood. A huge glass door in the motel was blown to pieces. The sky was dark and angry. Yet within a quarter of an hour everything had changed. It was perfectly calm. The sky was brilliantly blue. We could have gone out and sunbathed again! Where did the wind come from? How did it work? Where did it go? We had no idea! As A. W. Pink puts it, 'The wind is irresponsible; that is to say, it is sovereign in its action'.

In the same way, the Holy Spirit moves like a mighty wind according to God's sovereign and perfect will, and no man can understand how or why he does so. I remember conducting a campaign in the town of Ballymoney in Northern Ireland on one occasion. When I arrived in the Province, I was met at the airport and driven north into Co. Antrim. As we drove along, my host and I began to speak about Ireland's great spiritual history, and especially about the days of the revivals. He told me that we were at that moment driving through an area where God had moved in a remarkable way, with many hundreds being converted. Suddenly, as we approached a major road junction, he said 'You see this crossroad? The revival turned left here'. I was flabbergasted! 'You can't mean that!' I said. 'I mean exactly that,' he replied. 'From here on, and right through the next town,

15

the revival had no effect at all, but immediately beyond the town it broke out again.' I was speechless, struck dumb by an awesome sense of the mysterious power of God, that moved like a mighty wind according to his own sovereign will. Here was something that man could neither control nor organise. It was God on the loose – mighty, majestic, and *mysterious*!

'But,' says somebody, 'that is revival, which is something unique. Surely this mysterious working of the Holy Spirit is not true in the case of every individual conversion?' Yes it is! – and that is precisely the point that Jesus was making to Nicodemus. Here are his words again – '. . . so it is with *every one* who is born of the Spirit'. Every one – without exception! If you do not believe this, let me ask you a question. Can you tell me how you were born again? Now you may be able to tell me when, and where, and in what circumstances. You may be able to tell me under whose ministry you were converted, or even the text that gripped you. But can you tell me *how* it was done? Can you tell me how the Spirit opened your blind eyes to see the truth? . . . or how he unstopped your deaf ears to hear the Word of God? . . . or how he breathed life into your dead soul? Let me take it a step further. If you were converted in some kind of meeting, can you tell me how or why *you* were saved and the person next to you was not? Can you analyse what happened? The simple answer is that you cannot. The whole thing is a mystery! The operation of the Holy Spirit in the miracle of the new birth is mysterious.

Secondly, the objects are mysterious.

Now I know that some Christians are mysterious objects, but that is not quite the point I want to make here! Let us go back to a verse we noted earlier from the first Epistle of John – 'See what love the Father has given us, that we should be called children of God' (1 John 3.1). In the New International Version, the word 'given' is translated 'lavished', which helps to bring home the wonder of what John is saying. God has *lavished* his love upon us. Upon *us*, of all people, with all of our sin, rebellion, pride, impurity and selfishness! How amazing that in spite of the kind of people

16

we were, God lavished his love upon us, drew us to himself, forgave us our sin, and gave us the title 'children of God'! This is what I mean when I say that the objects of the new birth are mysterious. By any human reckoning or yardstick, we would never give that degree of honour to the kind of person we were. We choose the lovely, and reject the unlovely. I remember travelling by train in the North of England when, at one of the stations, a rather scruffy man came and sat in the same compartment. Soon, he began to talk . . . and talk . . . and talk! He made a voluble Frenchman sound like a deaf mute! Next, he started smoking at the same furious rate. Then the talking and the smoking combined to produce a bout of coughing that nearly rattled the windows. As if this was not enough, he began to excavate his nose in a way that is not recommended at highclass garden parties! And finally, he capped it all by taking his teeth out! I must say that I found it rather difficult to feel an overwhelming sense of love towards him: in fact, I could hardly wait to get off the train!

Yet no illustration can possibly make us understand the wonderful love of God for you and me while we were rebels against his authority and his law. As Paul says 'God shows his love for us in that *while we were yet sinners* Christ died for us' (Romans 5.8). When there was nothing good to be seen in us, and not a good word to be said for us, God loved us sufficiently to send his Son into the world to save us and bring us to himself. Charles H. Gabriel put his own sense of wonder like this:

> I stand all amazed at the love Jesus offers me;
> Confused at the grace that so fully he proffers me.
> I tremble to know that for me he was crucified –
> That for me, a sinner, he suffered, and bled, and died.

> Oh, it is wonderful that he should care for me!
> Enough to die for me!
> Oh, it is wonderful, wonderful to me.

But here is an even greater mystery. The Bible says that God set his love upon us *even before we were born!* Paul writes

'Blessed be the God and Father of our Lord Jesus Christ, who has blessed us in Christ with every spiritual blessing in the heavenly places, even as he chose us in him before the foundation of the world, that we should be holy and blameless before him' (Ephesians 1.3–4). The mystery deepens – and has no explanation! God has loved us, chosen us, called us to himself, forgiven our sins, and given us authority to be called his sons, and not one of us can understand, explain or analyse why or how he should do so. We can argue theology until the cows come home, but ultimately we reach a point where we are 'lost in wonder, love and praise'. Isaac Watts puts it beautifully in one of his marvellous hymns:

> Almighty God, to thee be endless honours done,
> The undivided Three, and the mysterious One.
> Where reason fails, with all her powers,
> There faith prevails and love adores!

2. THE MIRACLE OF BEING A SON OF GOD.

Becoming a son of God is not only a mystery – it is also a miracle. Let me take you back to Northern Ireland. I was once preaching in a youth campaign there, and God began to work in a wonderful way. A number of teens and twenties professed conversion, and soon the news began to filter through the town. Older people, including a number of married couples, began to come along to the informal coffee-bar meetings we were holding in the Town Hall. When I had finished preaching one night, one of the ministers organising the campaign introduced me to two men from his congregation. They were good-living, religious, respectable men in the town, but, as he told me quite bluntly in their presence, 'They are not saved; have a go at them!' The Irish are delightfully frank! We began to talk, and one of the men told me very honestly where he thought he stood spiritually. He was religious, a regular attender at the church, a member of the choir. He read his Bible, he prayed, he tried to be an honest businessman and a good husband – but he knew that he was not a Christian. Yet as he talked it was quite obvious that he genuinely wanted to become one and that he was looking for a missing link, for one little step that would take him over the line and into the Kingdom. When he had finished talking I looked him straight in the eye and said 'In spite of all that you have told me about your religion and respectability and goodness and sincerity, I want to tell you that there is only one thing you need. But it is not a little thing. Nor is it something that you can do. What you need is a miracle'. His reaction was to back away for a moment, but soon he began to emphasise how close he was to being saved, and how well he knew the gospel, and surely only one small step was needed to make him a Christian. But the more he spoke along those lines, the more I emphasised that he needed a miracle if he were to be saved, and that only God could perform that miracle. Gradually, the Lord opened his eyes to the truth, and later that evening, sitting in my parked car, the miracle happened, and that man was born again. He came to the point where he realised that what was needed was not a small step by him, but a great miracle by God – and when he reached there, and cried out to God to save him, God moved in and the miracle was performed.

What was true of that man (whose wife was converted soon afterwards) is true of every Christian. Each one begins his spiritual life with the new birth – and the new birth is a miracle. It is tremendously important to grasp this. A man can tidy up his old life, but he can never acquire a new one. He cannot buy it, earn it, or create it. As Jesus told Nicodemus, 'That which is born of the flesh is flesh, and that which is born of the Spirit is spirit' (John 3.6). Do you have any sense of wonder that your spiritual life is the result of a miracle? Are you so caught up with being a Christian that you have forgotten how you became one? Are you so busy trying to do things for the Lord that you are no longer overawed by what he has done for you? If so, let us try to get things in perspective by looking at an incident concerning the early disciples.

In Luke 10, there is a report of a staff conference that

Jesus had with the seventy disciples whom he had sent out on some form of evangelistic outreach. This is how Luke reports it: 'The seventy returned with joy, saying "Lord, even the demons are subject to us in your name!" And he said to them, "I saw Satan fall like lightning from heaven. Behold, I have given you authority to tread upon serpents and scorpions, and over all the power of the enemy; and nothing shall hurt you. Nevertheless do not rejoice in this, that the spirits are subject to you; but rejoice that your names are written in heaven" ' (Luke 10.17–20). Now it is interesting to notice that the word 'authority' is the word we looked at earlier in John 1.12, the Greek word *exousia*. Jesus had given the disciples unique authority to cast out evil spirits and to work miracles in his name, and when they returned we can just imagine them falling over each other to give their reports! They were just bursting to tell of the crowds, the meetings, the response, the miracles, and so on. And when they had poured out all their news, Jesus said, as it were, 'Well, that is wonderful. But there is something over which you can rejoice in an even greater way, and that is that *your* names are written in heaven'.

There is a great lesson here. We should never allow ourselves to be so caught up with the work we are doing that we lose sight of the wonder of what we have become. Ability in service is not as great a cause for rejoicing as authority in status. Of course it is wonderful to hear Christians speaking of the way in which the Lord has blessed their ministry, but there is always a danger that the emphasis can so easily become 'their ministry' and not 'the Lord'. The danger of dwelling too long on our Christian service is that we soon begin to speak as if we had done it by ourselves. The best antidote I know is to spend even longer rejoicing that our names are written in heaven, because we can be quite sure that we did nothing to contribute to that! And as Paul says of our salvation, 'Then what becomes of our boasting? It is excluded' (Romans 3.27).

Ability in service, over which people can so easily become boastful, is not as great a cause for rejoicing as authority in status, about which we cannot boast at all! And as a

Christian, you have the status of being a child of God. When did you last marvel and meditate on the wonder of that fact? John Newton was a blasphemous and godless slave-trader, but he was dramatically converted, and later entered the Church of England ministry. When he became the curate at Olney, in Buckinghamshire, he had parts of two verses of Scripture written above the mantelpiece in his study, the first from Isaiah 43.4, and the second from Deuteronomy 15.15. Put together, they read like this: 'Since thou wast precious in my sight, thou hast been honourable. . . . And thou shalt remember that thou wast a bondman in the land of Egypt, and the Lord thy God redeemed thee'. And whenever John Newton got away from the crowds, and the noise of his increasing fame, and knelt in his study alone, he had before him these words that reminded him that although he had been gripped by the slavery of his own sin, he had been precious in God's sight, and that in his wonderful and mysterious love, he had redeemed him and brought him to himself.

Find a place on the mantelpiece of your mind for that kind of truth! It will keep before you the wonderful fact that not only was your new birth into the Christian family a mystery that you cannot understand, it was also an amazing miracle that you could not undertake.

3. THE MARK OF BEING A SON OF GOD.

We began this study by saying that spiritual life began with spiritual birth. We can now put that another way by saying that the new birth is always followed by a new life. There is no such thing in the Bible as conversion without change, nor a person who has become a Christian but whose life remains the same in its moral quality. As Paul puts it so clearly, 'Therefore, if any one is in Christ, he is a new creation; the old has passed away, behold the new has come' (2 Corinthians 5.17). In other words the Christian is identified or marked out by a quality of life utterly different from the one he lived before he was converted.

I once took a week of meetings in a little log church in

Idaho up in the North-West of America. Every night I noticed in the congregation an old man who always wore a very striking bow tie. One night he told me something of his spiritual experience, and I discovered that the bow tie was not just used to keep his shirt from falling open! He told me that as a young man he led a rather wild life, and, amongst other things, was a slave to alcohol. Often when he was drunk he became violently sick, and his very wide ties – they were in fashion at the time - were right in the target area for 'matters arising'! Then he was suddenly and dramatically converted. The power of drink was broken, and, as he put it to me, 'I promised the Lord that I would never wear an ordinary tie again. My bow tie is a reminder to me that I have put off the old life and put on the new life. It is a mark of my conversion!'

That old man's testimony took me straight to Paul's letter to the Colossians, where he says to the Christians there – '. . . now is the time to cast off and throw away all these rotten garments of anger, hatred, cursing and dirty language. Don't tell lies to each other; it was your old life with all its wickedness that did that sort of thing; now it is dead and gone. You are living a brand new life that is ever learning more and more of what is right, and trying to be more and more like Christ who created this new life within you' (Colossians 3.8–10, Living Bible). God has given us a new spiritual wardrobe and he wants us to throw away the rotten rags we wore before we were converted. Now that we are Christians, what matters is not the character of our outward clothing, but the clothing of our inward character. A man may be poor or uneducated, or low down some people's social scale. He may be far from robust physically and have no obvious gifts of leadership. But the all-important thing is that he should bear clear-cut marks of being a child of God and be, as Paul puts it, 'trying to be *more and more like Christ* who created this new life within you'.

To put that in another way, what Paul is saying is that God's children should bear the family likeness. Jesus emphasises this in the Sermon on the Mount; 'You have

22

heard that it was said "You shall love your neighbour and hate your enemy". But I say to you, Love your enemies and pray for those who persecute you, *so that you may be sons of your Father who is in heaven*; for he makes his sun rise on the evil and on the good, and sends rain on the just and on the unjust' (Matthew 5.43–45). Now of course Jesus is not saying that by behaving in a certain way a man *becomes* a child of God. That would mean that we were justified by works and not by grace. The meaning is brought out in the Amplified Bible which translates this phrase 'to show that you *are* the children of your Father who is in heaven' – that is to say, by showing the family likeness in your behaviour. Now do you see the close link with the earlier part of our study? It was while we were sinners that God showed his love to us in sending Christ to die for us. Paul underlines this yet again when he says that 'while we were enemies we were reconciled to God by the death of his Son . . .' (Romans 5.10). It was when we were in open rebellion against God that he lavished his saving love upon us. When we were worth nothing, he gave us everything. He loved us even when he could not look upon us. That is how God acted towards us, and we are called upon to demonstrate the fact that we are his children by taking the same attitude towards all men, even our enemies. Of course we cannot save them, any more than we could save ourselves, but we are to act in love towards them regardless of how they act towards us. That is the point Jesus is making when he says that God sends sun and rain on good and evil men alike. God pours out these blessings on all men without distinction, upon the downright sinner as well as the upright saint. His gifts to men are not governed by their gifts to him. What moves God to act is what Dr. Martyn Lloyd-Jones has called 'His own eternal heart of love unmoved by anything outside itself'. The mark of a son of God is that more and more his actions towards his fellow-men, even his enemies, are governed not by what these other people say, or do, or think, but by the love of God poured into his heart by the Holy Spirit. That is the mark of being a son of God! Is there much of it in your life? Is your behaviour marked by a loving concern even for those who oppose you? Do you pray for those who persecute you? Do you overcome evil with good? Do you constantly seek the highest good even of those people whose temperament prevents you ever liking them? These are searching questions – but every professing Christian needs to face up to them. Only as you measure up to their demands will people take notice of your claim to be a child of God.

Chapter 2

A Saint

'ITALY TOPS THE SAINTS IN PARADISE LEAGUE'. That was the *Daily Telegraph* headline over an article that appeared in January 1974. A survey carried out by a Dutch Jesuit priest showed that of 1,848 'registered' saints, 626 were Italians. France came second with 576, while the British Isles eased into bronze medal position with 271. Other revealing statistics of what was called 'official paradise' showed that over 1,000 of these saints were Catholic priests during their time on earth, but that their number also included 15 ex-Popes, 14 former married women and eight widowers.

All fascinating stuff! – but a long way from biblical truth. According to the Bible, to describe a person as a 'saint' is just another way of calling him a Christian. In other words, the Bible says that every Christian in the world today is a saint. Writing to the Thessalonians, Paul warns of terrible judgment that will be inflicted on the ungodly at the second coming of Christ, 'when he comes on that day to be glorified in his saints, and to be marvelled at in all who have believed' (2 Thessalonians 1.10). Notice that Paul uses two phrases to describe certain people – 'his saints', and 'all who have believed'. But it is perfectly obvious that both refer to the same people. Saints are the people who have believed; those who have believed are saints. In other words, every Christian is a saint.

Now there are some biblical descriptions of a Christian that we are prepared to use quite freely about ourselves. We would gladly call ourselves believers, for instance, or servants, or even children of God – but we are a little reluctant to call ourselves saints! When did you last hear somebody say 'I am a saint'? Somehow, it sounds wrong. Boastful. Arrogant. We have a subconscious feeling that a saint is a particularly good Christian, a kind of honours graduate in Christian living, someone whose vastly superior quality of life warrants such a name. Yet that is thoroughly unbiblical and has robbed us of a whole storehouse of truth implicit in the use of the word 'saint' in the Bible. In this study, I want us, as it were, to recover the stolen property, by looking at three things that are implied by the fact that the Bible describes all Christians as saints.

1. OUR RELATIONSHIP TO THE LORD.

The Greek word translated 'saint' in our Bibles is the word *hagios*, which is often also translated as 'holy'. The Hebrew equivalent is used over 800 times in the Old Testament, where it usually has the primary meaning of 'separated', 'different', 'cut off' or 'set apart'. It is important to grasp this clearly before we go any further. The word's basic root does not refer to moral goodness as opposed to evil. It has to do not so much with the quality as with the nature of a thing. We can confirm this by a look at some of the ways and circumstances in which it occurs.

It is used of an article.

God's instructions to Moses at Sinai included the following: 'And you shall make *holy* garments for Aaron your brother, for glory and for beauty' (Exodus 28.2). The point about these garments was not that they were to be *cleaner* than any others (though I am sure they were clean) but that they were to be *different*. The material, the design, the

25

ornamentation, were all to mark out Aaron as holding a specific office in the affairs of the people.

It is used of a place.

Part of the tabernacle was called 'the *holy* place' (Leviticus 16.2), not because it was more hygienic than any other part of the tabernacle, but because it was curtained off from the remainder of the building.

It is used of a period of time.

In the story of creation, we read 'So God blessed the seventh day and *hallowed* it, because on it God rested from all his work which he had done in creation' (Genesis 2.3). The word 'hallowed' here is from the same root as 'holy', and again, the suggestion is not that that day was any better than any other, but rather that it was different. God performed all his mighty works of creation on the first six days, but on the seventh day he acted differently. He rested – and the seventh day was immediately marked out from the other six.

Now there is an obvious link between these three things. Aaron's garments were made differently at God's command; the holy place was cut off from the remainder of the tabernacle according to God's blueprint; the sabbath became different by God's decree. All of these things were different *because God himself is different*. He is utterly separate and apart from the whole of his universe. In Isaiah 40.25 we read: 'To whom then will you compare me, that I should be like him? says the Holy One'. And of course there is no answer to the question! God is incomparable – his very name and nature tell us that he is holy, different, separate from all others. When Isaiah had his amazing vision of the Lord, he spoke of celestial beings crying one to another and saying 'Holy, holy, holy is the Lord of hosts; the whole earth is full of his glory' (Isaiah 6.3). Only in the last book of the Bible (Revelation 4.8) do we again find a description of God, as it were, raised to the power of three, and the word that is used in this way is the word 'holy'. In their cry of adoration, the seraphim were acknowledging that God was, as Isaiah himself put it, 'high and lifted up' (Isaiah 6.1), utterly and essentially removed from every other being in the whole

26

universe. (Of course the word does also carry an ethical meaning, and when used of God it can only mean his perfection in every way.)

Turning to the New Testament, it is interesting to see that exactly the same word is used about all three Persons in the Godhead. In his wonderful prayer in John 17, Jesus prayed 'And now I am no more in the world, but they are in the world, and I am coming to thee. *Holy Father*, keep them in thy name, which thou hast given me, that they may be one, even as we are one' (John 17.11). A little later, when the disciples met for praise and prayer after the release of Peter and John from prison, they prayed that they might be given great boldness to preach in the face of their enemies 'while thou stretchest out thy hand to heal, and signs and wonders are performed through the name of *thy holy servant Jesus*' (Acts 4.30). When we come to the Third Person in the Godhead, there is no need to quote specific texts, because he is almost invariably described as 'the Holy Spirit'.

Here, then, is the great, characteristic word used about God. He is holy, different, separate from all else and from all others; and this is where we must begin if we are to have a biblical understanding of what it is to be 'holy', or to be 'a saint'. It is principally a matter of a special relationship with God. To go back to our three illustrations: Aaron's garments were to be used exclusively for God's worship. The holy place was set aside for that same sacred purpose. The seventh day was to be a unique opportunity for acknowledging the Lord's glory and showing forth his praise. These things were called 'holy' because of their relationship to God.

The same is true when the word 'saint' is used about people. It speaks firstly of relationship. When a person becomes a Christian, he becomes a saint, because he enters into a new, vital and personal relationship to God. In my home island of Guernsey there is a beautiful cove called Saints Bay a name we natives always abbreviate to 'Saints'. I remember an occasion when I caught a bus from St. Peter Port to go to Saints. As the bus drew away, two or three people came running towards the terminus. Our driver

27

leaned out of the window and shouted 'Saints?' 'No thank you' the people shouted back as they made for another bus. Accelerating away, the driver turned to us and said laughingly, 'Then they must be sinners'. This does not prove that all Guernsey bus drivers are theologians – but at least one made a precise biblical point at that moment! Every person in the world is either a saint or a sinner – and the saints are those who have come into a living relationship with God through faith in Jesus Christ.

It is interesting to contrast the biblical picture of a person becoming a saint with the one traditionally taught by the Roman Catholic Church. In the first place, the church canonises a person only after death; but the Bible says that a person becomes a saint while still alive. Traditional Catholic teaching is that a saint is elected by the church; whereas a biblical saint is chosen by the Lord. Thirdly, an ecclesiastical saint is made as the result of good works; the Bible teaches that a person is made a saint in spite of bad works. Fourthly, in the creating of a saint, the church looks for miracles worked by the person concerned; in the Bible, we are taught that a person becomes a saint because of a miracle worked *in* the person concerned. What a contrast! In the one case, the all-important thing is recognition by the church; in the other, the all-important thing is relationship to the Lord. What a complicated mess man gets into when he strays from the simplicity and beauty of the Gospel!

To return to our point: almost every time the word 'saint' is used in the Old Testament, there is a statement or inference about his relationship to the Lord. Saints are said to belong eternally to God. As David puts it, 'For the Lord loves justice; he will not forsake his saints' (Psalm 37.28). Whatever life's circumstances, the Christian can rest in the assurance of the Lord's over-ruling case. And when death comes? The Bible has a word for that too, for it says 'Precious in the sight of the Lord is the death of his saints' (Psalm 116.15). On a human level, of course, death is a very solemn thing, and Christians are in no way exempt from natural sorrow. But the Bible teaches that we need never

28

grieve over the death of a Christian 'as others do who have no hope' (1 Thessalonians 4.13) because of our assurance that at death the Christian passes into the presence of the Lord. While for us, on a human level, that person's death may be painful, for God, on a divine level, it is described as 'precious', because one of his saints, one of his children, one of those for whom Christ died, has come home, to be in his immediate and wonderful presence for ever. The saint's relationship with the Lord is one that lasts throughout life, through death, and into eternity. This is the first thing the Bible teaches us about being saints – our relationship to the Lord.

2. OUR DISCIPLESHIP IN THE WORLD.

It would be fascinating to go through the Bible with a fine tooth-comb to discover how many things we are told about the character, nature and attributes of God. Yet we could summarize them all in just three words. It would be equally interesting to discover how many commandments, both negative and positive, the Bible gives to Christians. They must run into hundreds – yet they, too, could be summarized in three words. What is more, we can take the three words that sum up everything the Bible says about God's character, and the three words that sum up all the Bible's moral demands on the Christian, and find them all in just one verse! – the one where God says 'Be ye holy, for I am holy' (1 Peter 1.16 AV). It would be impossible to put a description of God and a summary of his demands upon men into fewer words than that. We already have many versions of the Bible – the Authorised Version, the Revised Version, the Amplified Version and so on - but this is what we could call the transistorised version! The simplest way to describe God is to say that he is holy, and the simplest way to describe his requirements for us is to say that he commands us to be holy. Commenting on this verse in 1 Peter, Alan Stibbs wrote: 'So the first and sufficient reason why God's people should keep themselves from uncleanness is because the Lord their God is holy; only so can they

29

respond to their calling and enjoy intimate fellowship with him. It is, therefore, the revelation of God's character and the call to be intimately related to him that makes holiness an obligation'. I like that! Our discipleship is demanded by the very nature of the one with whom we are in such a wonderful relationship. When a young Christian asks 'But why should I behave differently from my unconverted friends?' the answer is 'Because you *are* different!' In other words, Scripture demands that your practice should correspond to your position. Because you are a saint, you should become saintly. As Matthew Henry once put it: ' "Be ye holy" is the great and fundamental law of our religion'.

Let us pursue that, negatively and positively:

Firstly, there is the negative aspect.

Paul writes to the Ephesians: 'Therefore be imitators of God, as beloved children. And walk in love, as Christ loved us and gave himself up for us, a fragrant offering and sacrifice to God. But immorality and all impurity or covetousness must not even be named among you, *as is fitting among saints.* Let there be no filthiness, nor silly talk, nor levity, *which are not fitting*; but instead let there be thanksgiving' (Ephesians 5.1–4). Do you see Paul's point? There are certain actions that are plainly not right for Christians. These things may be done by the world, and represent the normal social standards of the day – but a saint is different, and is to behave differently. I will never forget the first time I came across a phrase in 1 John 5.18. I was a young Christian, and whole areas of the Bible were new to me. This particular phrase really bowled me over: 'We know that any one born of God does not sin'. What did it mean? I was certainly not sinless – was I not a Christian at all? Then I discovered the tense and the meaning of the words used. John does not mean that a Christian never commits even one isolated act of sin. That would make nonsense of Christ's command to the disciples to pray 'Forgive us our sins' (Luke 11.2), and it would contradict what John himself says earlier in his first Epistle when he writes '... if any one does sin, we have an advocate

30

with the Father, Jesus Christ the righteous . . .' (1 John 2.1).
What the verse means is that the general tenor and thrust
and direction of a Christian's life is away from sin. He does
not gladly and habitually continue in sinful ways. I remember
discussing this verse with Mrs. Mary Wood, whose life and
ministry in the National Young Life Campaign has enriched
my life and the lives of countless other people. After we
had discussed the theological background and the Greek
tenses and all the other technicalities, she said to me 'John,
what this verse means is that for the Christian, *sin is not
the done thing!*' I can hardly improve on that! It is not the
done thing. It is out of character. Let me give a simple Old
Testament illustration. When Nehemiah was advised to
escape when his life was in danger, his reply was instant and
characteristic: 'Should such a man as I flee?' (Nehemiah
6.11). God had called him to stand firm; how could he run
away? His position demanded courage; how could he offer
cowardice? Nehemiah recognised that his behaviour must
be related to his divinely appointed position – and every
Christian should have a similar sense of discipleship and
discipline. Negatively, then, to be a saint means the
discipline of resisting temptation and rejecting sin at
every turn, because to do otherwise is to betray our
position.

Secondly, there is the positive aspect.

Paul tells the Thessalonians: 'For God did not call us to
be impure, but to live a holy life' (1 Thessalonians 4.7,
New International Version). Writing in the New Bible
Dictionary, Professor R. A. Finlayson says: 'The New
Testament everywhere emphasizes the ethical nature of
holiness in contrast to all uncleanness. It is represented as
the supreme vocation of Christians and the goal of their
living'. Here is the truth put positively and it is important
to stress that the Christian life *is* positive. The Christian's
code of conduct does include important negatives, as eight
of the Ten Commandments indicate – but the Christian life
is essentially a matter of positive goodness.

A minister who tended to major on 'Thou shalt not' took
morning service in a little country church, and later went to

31

lunch with a Christian farmer. After lunch, the farmer said 'I would like you to come and meet my donkey'. The preacher agreed, but asked why the farmer was so keen on the idea. 'Because my donkey is a Christian,' the farmer replied. 'Don't be ridiculous,' the preacher retorted, 'no donkey can be a Christian.' 'Well, according to your sermon this morning it can,' the farmer said. 'My donkey doesn't swear, drink alcohol, smoke tobacco or work on Sundays, and I reckon that according to your sermon it must be a Christian!' He might even have added that, by some standards, the donkey's long face was an added qualification! Christian discipleship is positive. A Christian should be seeking not merely to empty his life of sin, but to fill it with goodness. As the writer to the Hebrews says, we are to: 'strive to live in peace with everybody, and *pursue* that consecration and holiness without which no one will ever see the Lord' (Hebrews 12.14). Peter adds that if a man would know God's blessing on his life, '. . . let him turn away from evil *and do right*. . . .' (1 Peter 3.11). Positive Christian discipleship is the vocation to which we are called. John Newton once put it like this, in words which it would be impossible to better outside the Bible itself: 'Christ has taken our nature into heaven, to represent us, and has left us on earth, with his nature, to represent him'. To be a saint not only means relationship to the Lord, it also demands discipleship in the world.

3. *FELLOWSHIP IN THE CHURCH.*

The word 'saint' is used over sixty times in the New Testament, and on every occasion except one it is in the plural. The only exception is where Paul tells the Philippian Christians to 'greet every saint in Christ Jesus', and as this obviously has a plural connotation – it means 'all the saints' – we have the remarkable fact that the word is never used of a person in isolation. The lesson is clear. No Christian is meant to go it alone, or 'do his own thing'. While it is true that every Christian comes to Christ as an individual, it is equally true that from the moment of his conversion he is in fellowship with every other Christian in the world. The Christian faith is intensely personal, but cannot ever be private. Paul has a wonderful chapter in Ephesians in which he describes the changes that come over a man when he is converted, and one of them is this: 'So then you are no longer strangers and sojourners, but you are fellow citizens with the saints and members of the household of God. . . .' (Ephesians 2.19).

This 'household of God' includes in its earthly members all Christians of all ages, all levels of intelligence, all nationalities, and all levels of social strata. As Paul puts it so marvellously: 'There is neither Jew nor Greek, there is neither slave nor free, there is neither male nor female; for you are all one in Christ Jesus' (Galatians 3.28). A preacher friend of mine was once taking a series of meetings in a place I know well – the town of Katerini in Macedonia, Northern Greece. One evening, he was on the verandah of the church orphanage photographing the sunset, when a Greek workman, whom he rightly took to be a Christian, happened to join him. The language barrier was impassable, but my friend was determined to do something to express the sense of fellowship that he felt in his heart. Pointing to the flaming glory of the sunset over the mountains, he looked at the workman and said 'Jesus!' Next, he pointed to the spire of the church a few yards away and said 'Jesus!' Then his arm pointed straight into the sky while he said yet again 'Jesus'. Finally, he put one hand over the workman's heart and his other hand over his own heart and repeated once more – 'Jesus'. Their backgrounds, cultures and languages could hardly have been more different – but in that moment they knew something much more significant, and that was that they were 'fellow-citizens with the saints'! Yet that striking encounter was something special. In those rather emotional circumstances, we might easily do the same kind of thing. The real test comes when we are on home ground, among Christians whose language (and background and circumstances and failings and business in general!) we know only too well. Sadly, somebody was not far from the truth when he wrote:

To dwell above with saints we love,
Oh my! That will be glory.
To dwell below, with saints we know,
Well, that's another story!

As we have seen, the Bible tells us that we are '*all* one in Christ Jesus' – and that includes that old fuddy-duddy who sits two rows in front of you in church, that brash teenager who acts if he and God were buddies, that hyper-spiritual lady who goes around gushing with glory, and that stick-in-the-mud deacon who does not have the intelligence to agree with you on the obvious solution to your church's problems! It is here, at the grass-roots, local level, that we are called upon to demonstrate the reality of our oneness in Christ, and we will not do it by repeating slogans to each other. The real challenge is to demonstrate the reality of our fellowship by such things as sympathy, understanding, prayer, ready forgiveness, reluctance to criticise, practical help when it is needed and not merely when it is asked for, and a willingness to act as a family in dealing with individual and corporate needs in the church. As William Hendriksen puts it: 'Everybody should put his shoulder under the burdens under which this or that individual member is groaning, whatever these burdens may be. They must be carried jointly'.

What a vast area of thought that opens up! The need may be for money, help in looking after children in an emergency, home care for an invalid, sympathy and understanding in an hour of grief, unjudging help in recovering from a moral fall. The list is endless – and the call is obvious! The fact of our fellowship makes inevitable, practical and inescapable demands upon us. We are saints *together*.

I sometimes receive letters from Christians who sign off with the phrase 'Yours because his'. That is wonderfully and profoundly true. As Christians, we belong to each other because we first belong to the Lord. In other words our fellowship in the church is directly linked to our relationship to the Lord. Paul not only told the Ephesian Christians that they were 'members of his (Christ's) body' (Ephesians

34

5.30); he also reminded them that 'we are members one of another' (Ephesians 4.25). Writing to the Christians at Rome, he put both truths in one sentence, when he said that '. . . we, though many, are one body in Christ, and individually members one of another' (Romans 12.5). That one verse speaks not only of our wonderful privilege as Christians, it also tells us of our deep, searching responsibility to every other Christian in the world, regardless of race, colour, age or denomination. We are bound to each other in a fellowship that goes far beyond the mere sharing of a common interest, hobby, or political affiliation. It is a supernatural and spiritual reality that carries with it the responsibility of Christlike, caring love.

Only when we learn to enjoy that kind of fellowship, show that kind of love, and bear each others burdens in such a sympathetic way, will we be fulfilling our vocation as saints.

Chapter 3

A Sheep

Have you ever seen a sheep giving an impersonation of a horse or a donkey? It is not a pretty sight, especially when the sheep has only two legs! To unravel this conundrum, we need to go to the heart of the Old Testament where God gives this unusual command: 'Be not like a horse or a mule, without understanding . . .' (Psalm 32.9). What a vivid picture! A horse is an impetuous, headstrong animal, always wanting to plunge forward in its own way; whereas a mule, or a donkey, is always wanting to dig in its heels, obstinately refusing to budge. That particular part of the Psalm is about being guided by God in one's daily life, and the point being made is that if a Christian wants to walk with God he must neither dash ahead in impetuous enthusiasm, nor lag behind in hesitant unbelief. He must be willing to ask and wait for the Lord's leading – and then obey without hesitation. In other words, the Christian must not act like a horse or a donkey! – and what makes that kind of behaviour even more out of place is that one of the Bible's great names for a Christian is not a horse or a mule . . . but a sheep! It is this particular picture of a Christian that we are going to study in this chapter. The picture of the Christian as a sheep is used in the Psalms, in Isaiah, in Ezekiel, and in several places in the New Testament – but in this study I want us to concentrate on John 10, with occasional reference to the best-known passage in the Old Testament, Psalm 23.

The first thing to notice is that these passages have the same focal point, or centre of gravity. The more you read them, the more obvious it becomes that they are not essentially about the sheep, but about the shepherd. In John 10, this is crystallised in Jesus's words 'I am the good shepherd' (v. 11). In Psalm 23, everything stems from the opening words, 'The Lord is my shepherd'. The emphasis in both places is not on what the sheep ought to do, but on what the shepherd has done and is doing for the sheep. There is not a single instruction in either passage; not one thing that we are told to do or not to do. Both passages are a wonderful exposition of the Good Shepherd's activities on behalf of his sheep, his careful and loving provision for them. In this study we are going to look at some of these activities and at what they should mean to us in our daily lives.

1. SALVATION.

This is beginning at the beginning! The first thing the shepherd provides for his sheep is salvation. In the early part of Jesus' earthly ministry, we read that 'When he saw the crowds, he had compassion on them, because they were harassed and helpless, like sheep without a shepherd' (Matthew 9.36). There are two ways of getting at the truth of what this means. The first is to take a closer look at the words that are used to describe the crowds. The word translated 'harassed' includes the sense of being bewildered and confused, of not knowing which way to turn. The word translated 'helpless' literally means 'thrown down'. It is a picture of people depressed, dejected and demoralised. Jesus saw that these people were confused and helpless. The second way of understanding what is being said here is by using the very illustration that the verse gives. We are told that Jesus saw the crowds 'like sheep without a shepherd'. In the Middle East, a shepherd is usually the owner of a very small flock of sheep which he *leads* from one place to another. Notice that! In fertile lands, and certainly here in Britain, the shepherd *follows* the sheep. Providing fresh pasture is usually just a question of transferring them from one grassy field into the next. All the shepherd has to do is to open a gate and encourage the sheep to drift in that general direction. But in the Middle East the picture is quite different. Green pasture is scattered and scarce, and the sheep have no instinct as to where it can be found. What happens is that the shepherd, with his knowledge of the area, goes in front, finds the pastures and watering places and then leads the sheep to them.

Now the illustration is becoming clear. To put it bluntly, without a shepherd, the sheep would be mutton! No shepherd - no grass; no grass – no food; no food - no life. It is literally true that for the sheep, the shepherd means life. And Jesus saw the people around him 'like sheep without a shepherd'! They were spiritually dead. Without him they were without hope. Here is a fundamental truth. The first thing that the shepherd gives the sheep is life. When Jesus said 'I am come that they might have life. . . .' (John 10.10), he did not merely mean that he had come to give a new dimension to life, or to guide men's lives into new avenues of usefulness – *he came to give them life*. Let us be absolutely clear on this point. Left to himself, man is spiritually dead, 'having no hope and without God in the world' (Ephesians 2.12). He has no spiritual sense of direction. Isaiah puts it perfectly when he says that 'All we like sheep have gone astray; we have turned every one to his own way' (Isaiah 53.6). The unconverted is deliberately off course. He has

37

chosen to die in a wilderness of his own making, and unless the Good Shepherd comes to his rescue he is doomed for ever. Only when we grasp this can we understand the importance of Jesus coming into the world. The birth, life, death, and resurrection of Jesus was not just an elaborate publicity campaign for higher moral standards; it was a rescue mission. As Paul puts it so clearly: 'And you he made alive, when you were dead through the trespasses and sins in which you once walked. . . .' (Ephesians 2.1–2).

Going back to John 10, we find the additional and amazing truth that Jesus secured the Christian's life at the cost of his own. As Jesus himself puts it: 'The good shepherd lays down his life for the sheep' (v. 11), and again, 'I lay down my life for the sheep' (v. 15). Jesus did not come into the world on some vague goodwill enterprise. He came for the specific and pre-determined purpose of dying in the place of 'the sheep', of his people, in order that their sins might be put away and that they might receive the gift of eternal life. The angel's prophecy to Mary before the birth of Jesus was clear and definite: '. . . you shall call his name Jesus, for he *will* save his people from their sins' (Matthew 1.21). Nothing was left to chance. The death of Christ was not a proposition to sinners, it was a plan of salvation, and because it was God's plan, it worked! With unerring certainty, the Holy Spirit draws to faith in Christ all those for whom he died, so that every Christian in the world can echo the words of Phillip Bliss's great hymn:

> Bearing shame and scoffing rude,
> In my place condemned he stood;
> Sealed my pardon with his blood:
> Hallelujah! What a Saviour!

Are you rejoicing in that certainty? Are you sure that he died in *your* place, bearing *your* sin? Can you say with David 'The Lord is *my* Shepherd'? This is where the Christian life begins!

2. SENSITIVITY.

Secondly, the Good Shepherd gives his sheep sensitivity;

notice several references to this in John 10. First, Jesus uses the natural illustration, and says that when the shepherd comes to the communal sheepfold, 'the sheep hear his voice' (v. 3). He then goes on to say that when the shepherd has collected all his own sheep, 'he goes before them, and the sheep follow him, for they know his voice. A stranger they will not follow, but they will flee from him, for they do not know the voice of strangers' (vv. 4–5). Later on, he applies this truth spiritually, and says 'My sheep hear my voice, and I know them, and they follow me. . . .' (v. 27).

These verses are all speaking about sensitivity, and when we consider this as something given to us by the Lord, it becomes very significant and wonderful.

Firstly, it is true in salvation.

Did you come to Christ the very first time you heard the gospel? Almost certainly not. You probably heard the gospel many times before you became a Christian. But there came a wonderful day when you heard, not only with your outward ears, but with what we could call your spiritual ears. The Lord made you receptive to the message which you had previously rejected. He tuned you into the truth of the gospel message. He made you sensitive to his voice. Let me focus the picture a little more closely. If you were converted in a meeting or service, there may have been many other people present who heard exactly the same preacher, sang the same hymns, joined in the same prayers. Some were Christians, but others were not. Can you explain why some of those people were utterly unmoved by what was said, while for you it led to a miracle? Can you explain why you said 'Yes' to Christ while they said 'No'? The difference lay here: they heard the preacher's words, but you heard the Lord's voice. And the reason you were able to hear that voice, and recognise it, and respond to it, was that the Lord himself made you sensitive to it.

The New Testament story of Lydia's conversion is a clear illustration of this. Paul and Silas were in Philippi as part of an evangelistic tour, and attended an open-air meeting by the riverside. As they shared the gospel with the people, one of those who heard them was a local tradeswoman by the name of Lydia. As Paul was preaching we read that 'The Lord opened her heart to give heed to what was said by Paul' (Acts 16.14). In other words, the Lord gave her sensitivity. He graciously enabled her to understand the significance of what was being said, and to respond to it in repentance and faith. I have heard some preachers give the impression that the sinner has the power to open his own heart with, as it were, poor little Jesus standing outside in frustrated suspense, waiting for the sinner to do him a favour. Nothing could be further from the truth! Every Christian should rejoice in the fact that the only way in which he was able to be saved was that, in his great mercy, the Lord gave him sensitivity to hear and understand the gospel.

Secondly, it is true in the matter of conscience.

Somebody once described conscience as 'A still, small voice that makes minority reports' – but deeper truth will help us more than that rather cynical remark! Moffatt translates Proverbs 20.27 like this: 'Man's conscience is the lamp of the Eternal, flashing into his inmost soul'. That is right on line with the Bible's general teaching that when a person becomes a Christian God gives him a sensitive conscience. The more a Christian grows in his knowledge of the Bible, and in the grace of God, the more clearly does he recognise the difference between right and wrong. Going back to the illustration from nature in John 10, the more mature a sheep becomes, the more clearly does it learn to recognise the voice of the shepherd, and to turn away from the voice of the dangerous stranger.

There is a story of a Christian who attended a conference held by Tom Rees at Hildenborough Hall. On the last day there was a testimony session, in which people were invited to share something of what they had learned during their time there. One man brought the house down by saying 'Mr. Rees, I just want you to know that I never realised what sin was until I came to Hildenborough Hall'! I can imagine what Tom Rees made of that! – but of course the man was making a very important point, namely that under the teaching of the Word of God he had become much more sensitive in his conscience. He had a much clearer picture of sin's seriousness, subtlety and power. Every Christian should seek to develop that kind of sensitivity. Pray for an increasing ability to recognise the voice of the Lord in your life, and to ignore the voice of any 'stranger' who would lead you into disobedience, danger or disgrace.

Thirdly, it is true in the question of understanding the Bible.
I am not suggesting that any Christian understands the meaning of every passage, phrase and word in the Bible – not even those who give the impression that they do! – but God does give Christians a spiritual understanding of his Word. One of the loveliest incidents in the New Testament records what happened to two disciples while they were walking to Emmaus on the first Easter Day. Suddenly, they were joined by Jesus, but did not recognise him. They talked together about the tremendous events of the previous days, and the disciples even told Jesus about reports of the tomb being empty. Finally, he began to explain to them why these momentous events were a necessary fulfilment of prophecy: 'And beginning with Moses and all the prophets, he interpreted to them in all the scriptures the things concerning himself' (Luke 24.27). After he had left them we read that 'They said to each other, "Did not our hearts burn within us while he talked to us on the road, while he opened to us the scriptures?" ' (Luke 24.32). Until the Lord opened their eyes, not even Christ's death and resurrection fitted into place.

Overwhelmed by what they now knew, they returned to Jerusalem to share the news with the other disciples. While they were telling their story, Jesus appeared again. After assuring them that he really had risen from the dead, he explained once more that his death and resurrection were an essential fulfilment of Old Testament prophecy and '. . . He opened their minds to understand the scriptures . . .' (Luke 24.45). In other words, he gave them sensitivity to the truth of the Bible.

It is wonderful to grasp what this means to you as a Christian! When Jesus was warning the disciples of his coming death, he promised them that after he had gone away into heaven they would receive the Holy Spirit, and went on to say that 'When the Spirit of truth comes, he will guide you into all truth . . .' (John 16.13). Through the Holy Spirit, God has promised to give Christians an understanding of his Word, a sensitivity to the truth. You may not be an expert, a scholar, or a theologian, but if you are a Christian, God has promised you the enabling of the Holy Spirit to understand his Word and to apply it to your heart and life. I know of nothing more exciting than to come away from the Bible knowing that God has spoken to me through its pages; that words written thousands of years ago have come alive for *me*, in my own life and circumstances. It is thrilling, electrifying! J. B. Phillips uses exactly that kind of picture in the Preface to his Letters to Young Churches (the Epistles) where he writes that while he was at work on this book '. . . again and again the writer felt rather like an electrician re-wiring an ancient house without being able to "turn the mains off" '. We should always be praying for that kind of sensitivity as we read the Bible. It is wonderful beyond words that in spite of our ignorance, our immaturity and all our other failures, we can turn to the Bible and hear the Lord's voice as clearly as if he were standing physically alongside us. That experience is not the result of reasoning, nor of research, but of revelation – God making himself known to us, giving us a sensitivity to his Word.

3. *SUSTENANCE.*

This is connected very closely to what we have just been studying. Going back once again to John 10, we find Jesus saying, 'I am the door; if any one enters by me, he will be saved, and will go in and out and find pasture' (v. 9). We can link that with Psalm 23, where David's testimony is '. . . he makes me lie down in green pastures. He leads me beside still waters . . .' (vv. 1–2). In physical life there are three essentials to good health – food (and drink), exercise and rest. These combine to provide sustenance for the body.

42

In a sense, our two passages give us spiritual parallels. For food and drink, we have 'green pastures' and 'still waters'; for exercise we 'go in and out'; and for rest 'he makes me to lie down'. Now while we could not press an exegesis of those phrases quite as closely as that, what *is* plain from these two passages, and wonderfully true as a living experience, is that the Lord, having saved his sheep, and having given them sensitivity to his voice, also provides all that they need for their daily spiritual sustenance.

No Christian ought to doubt that! Jesus is no mere part-time shepherd, hired to do a job but with no personal interest in the sheep. He is 'the Good Shepherd', who so loves the sheep that he gives his life for them. Is it likely that such a Shepherd would ever leave the sheep without sustenance? Paul asks the same kind of question when he writes to the Romans: 'What then shall we say to this? If God is for us, who is against us? He who did not spare his own Son but gave him up for us all, will he not also give us all things with him? (Romans 8.31–32). That section of Romans is written in the specific context of the Christian suffering in the world, and Paul reminds his readers that as far as the world is concerned '. . . we are regarded as sheep to be slaughtered' (Romans 8.36)! It is as he visualises the Christian defenceless and helpless against the attacks of the devil, the pressures of an evil world and the treachery of his own heart, that Paul assures him of God's gracious provision of 'all things'. The New English Bible puts it like this: 'He did not spare his own Son, but surrendered him for us all; and with this gift how can he fail to lavish upon us all he has to give'? That captures perfectly the spirit of what Paul is saying. We may feel as helpless as sheep in a world over-run by ravenous wolves, but as surely as the Good Shepherd has died to give us eternal life, just as surely is he with us day by day to provide our every need, and to 'lavish upon us all he has to give'. But we have a responsibility here. In another Psalm, David tells us 'Cast your burden on the Lord, and he will sustain you' (Psalm 55.22). God provides in answer to prayer. The Christian who gets out of touch with the Shepherd must not be surprised if he finds the supplies drying up! Now to a fourth thing the Good Shepherd supplies:

4. SATISFACTION.

This takes our last point a little further. We could say that satisfaction speaks of a conscious enjoyment of God's goodness. Let us go back to our basic passages of scripture. Jesus says in John 10, '. . . I am come that they may have life, and have it abundantly' (v. 10) – or, as the Amplified Bible puts it, 'in abundance – to the full, till it overflows'. In Psalm 23, David says 'The Lord is my Shepherd, I shall not want', and adds '. . . my cup overflows'. Somebody once said 'There are two things I have always looked upon as difficult. The one is to make the wicked sad, and the other is to make the godly joyful'. What a tragic remark. There is something wrong with Christians who give the impression that godliness is measured by the darkness of your suit, or the length of your face. Of course there are Christians who go to the other extreme, and who seem to measure sanctification by smiles and godliness by grins, and who seem to be saying that unless you are singing a happy chorus all day long, and bubbling over with the prescribed amount of evangelical effervescence you are probably a backslider. That is nonsense, of course – but I am equally sure that every Christian in the world should seek for a deep, conscious and continuous enjoyment of the Lord in his heart. The first question asked in the Westminster Assembly's Shorter Catechism (1647) is 'What is the chief end of man?' The answer given is this: 'Man's chief end is to glorify God and to enjoy him for ever'. Every Christian should seek to live in the spirit of that reply!

No Christian ought to find life in today's world easy or undemanding, because he is living in an alien environment, and is surrounded by problems, tensions, trials, stresses, difficulties and temptations on every hand. But neither should he go round giving the impression that the Christian life is dull, burdensome, restrictive and unsatisfying. I can think of some Christians whose general demeanour is such that if I were unconverted I would not go within a mile of them, in case I caught what they had! We are meant to enjoy our salvation, not to endure it! The secret of living a responsible, caring life in today's world, and yet doing so with an inner radiance that commends our faith to others, is to allow nothing to come between us and a daily preoccupation with *the Lord himself*. The Psalmist says '*He* satisfies him who is thirsty, and the hungry he fills with good things' (Psalm 107.9). Notice my italics! This needs following through a little. There are many 'earthly pleasures' that we can genuinely enjoy – physical, mental, cultural, artistic, social, and so on, and these may be perfectly legitimate, honest and commendable.

It is the devil's lie that the worlds of music, art and sport, to name but three, are in a rather similar (but always undefined) way dangerously close to being 'worldly', part of a humanistic culture, but not things that can be wholly committed to the Lord or enjoyed with his unreserved blessing. That is nonsense! The Bible teaches quite plainly that God 'richly and ceaselessly provides us with everything for our enjoyment' (1 Timothy 6.17, Amplified Bible), and to limit the word 'everything' to the realm of the theological, or even the spiritual, is to become the impoverished victims of misguided zeal.

The simple and liberating truth is that 'Every good endowment and every perfect gift is from above, coming down from the Father of lights. . . .' (James 1.17) – and that includes those given to unconverted men, who, for all their unbelief are nevertheless 'made in the likeness of God' (James 3.9). To attempt to shut ourselves off from these gifts and these people is to refuse God's open-handed goodness because of our short-sighted prejudice.

But having said that, it remains true that no enjoyment of culture, the arts, sport and so on, can ever bring us complete *satisfaction* – for the simple reason that man is more than cultural, artistic and sporting. These activities may relax us, exhilarate us, or refresh us – but they can never satisfy us, even when they promise to do so. While playing at Black Mountain Golf Club, North Carolina (the golfing 'home' of Billy Graham) I came across this couplet in the professional's shop –

> My only wish afore I go to heaven
> Is to come in just once with a sixty-seven.

As a golfing enthusiast, every bone in my body aches to do just that! – but I know perfectly well that even if I did, it would not satisfy me. There is more to life than breaking par, and more to man's make-up than that which can find pleasure in culture, sport or the arts. Man is essentially *spiritual* and it is only at that level that he can ever find true satisfaction. Nor can he find that satisfaction in religious or Christian 'things'. Religious activities cannot produce it. We only find it when the Lord *himself* draws us by the Holy Spirit into a deep consciousness of our living fellowship with him and of his blessing on our lives. Jesus made the tremendous promise 'Blessed are those who hunger and thirst for righteousness, *for they shall be satisfied*' (Matthew 5.6). Do you know anything of that incessant spiritual appetite? Are you constantly longing to know more of the Lord and to live in utter obedience to his will? Only God can create those longings in your heart – and only he can satisfy them!

Now we come to the final word in our study of the Good Shepherd's provision for his sheep:

5. SECURITY.

This is one of the great themes in both John 10 and Psalm 23, and they speak of security in two ways:

Firstly, there is earthly security.

In John 10 Jesus speaks of the dangers to the flock when attacked by a wolf. He says that the hired hand would run away, leaving the flock to be ravaged, but goes on to assure us that 'I am the Good Shepherd' (v. 14), inferring that he will never leave us alone, unprotected and insecure. In Psalm 23 David says 'Thou preparest a table before me in the presence of my enemies . . .' (v. 5), and adds in the next verse, 'Surely goodness and mercy shall follow me all the days of my life' (v. 6). We could call this earthly security, the promise of God's presence and protection no matter how great our earthly enemies. When Adoniram Judson went as a missionary to Burma, he was captured by ruthless natives, strung up by his thumbs, tortured and then flung into a filthy prison cell. As he lay there, his captors taunted him: 'And what now of your plans to evangelize the heathen?' Judson's reply was simple and superb: 'My future is as bright as the promises of God'. Do you have the same kind of confidence in the goodness of God, and the faithfulness of his Word? Are you serenely certain of God's over-ruling and care when things go wrong? Are you absolutely convinced that 'No good thing does the Lord withhold from those who walk uprightly' (Psalm 84.11)? Look at Psalm 23 again. Have you ever noticed that David is not so much giving a word of testimony, but rather making a statement of faith? What he says is 'Goodness and mercy *shall* follow me all the days of my life'. He looks into an unknown future, and is convinced that there will never be a day when the goodness and mercy of God will not be his. That is what I call a sense of earthly security! Do you possess it?

Secondly, there is eternal security.

Again, both passages take up this theme. In John 10, Jesus says of his sheep '. . . and I give them eternal life, and they shall never perish, and no one shall snatch them out of my hand. My Father, who has given them to me, is greater than all, and no one is able to snatch them out of the Father's hand' (vv. 28–29); while David ends Psalm 23 by saying '. . . . and I shall dwell in the house of the Lord for ever' (v. 6). In John 10, the Shepherd makes the promise; in Psalm 23, the sheep claims it! What a wonderful blending of the two passages – but are they intended to have any practical effect on our lives as Christians? I believe they are, and so are all the other truths that we have examined in this study. You will remember that we noticed at the beginning of the chapter that there is not a single imperative, not one commandment, in either of the two main passages we are studying. All they do is to magnify the grace of God, show us his understanding of our needs; his love; his care; his provision. Has all of this produced any response in your heart? Let me remind you again of the things we have discovered.

Firstly, the Lord gave you salvation. By nature, you did not want it, by self-effort you could not achieve it, and by instinct you did not know where to find it. You were blind, and the Lord gave you sight; deaf, and he opened your ears; sick, and he made you whole; dead, and he brought you to life.

He gave you then, and continues to give you now, sensitivity to his voice. He quickens your conscience, enabling you to sense more and more the things that will be a blessing to you and the things that will harm you. He opens the eyes of your understanding as you read the Bible, so that you have a supernatural knowledge of spiritual truth, and can apply it to your daily life.

Then he sustains you. He provides all your spiritual needs, lavishing upon you all that he has to give. He restores your soul. He makes you to lie down in green pastures, and beside still waters.

What is more, he satisfies you at the deepest point of your being, fully meeting the most profound longings of heart and spirit. He gives you abundant life, so that your cup overflows.

Finally, he gives you earthly and eternal security, promising that goodness and mercy will follow you all the days of your life, and that you will dwell in the house of the Lord for ever, nobody or nothing being able to snatch you out of his hand. And whatever your failures, lack of understanding, doubts, fears, or anxieties, God has pledged that all of these things will remain yours as the gracious gifts of the Good Shepherd.

And what about the commandments, the laws, the thunders and the lightnings? Where are the warnings, the exhortations, the disciplines, the demands?

Are they always necessary? Of course there are times when nothing less than a solemn reminder of what Paul calls 'the severity of God' (Romans 11.22), or the inflexible demands of His moral law, will jolt us out of sin, indiscipline, carelessness or low-level living – but at other times God seeks to draw us closer to Himself by a whispered revelation of His amazing love and unfailing provision.

That is what He is doing here: what are you doing?

Chapter 4

A Stone

Many of the titles given to Christians in the Bible are repeated again and again. This is certainly true of those we have seen so far – a son, a saint, and a sheep. We are now going to study a title that occurs only once – yet which gives us an important part of the answer to our question 'What in the world is a Christian?' The word we are looking for is in a sentence from the first Epistle of Peter. This is how it reads:

'. . . like living stones be yourselves built into a spiritual house, to be a holy priesthood, to offer spiritual sacrifices acceptable to God through Jesus Christ' (1 Peter 2.5).

Peter tells us that a Christian is a stone, which on the face of it, hardly sounds very complimentary, because in the natural world a stone is inanimate and senseless! But a Christian stone is vastly different, as we shall discover by noticing four basic truths contained in this verse.

1. *THE TRANSFORMATION THAT IS EFFECTED.*

There can surely be little doubt that it was Peter who wrote this Epistle. If you glance at the end of Chapter 1 and the beginning of Chapter 2 you will see a whole torrent of ideas and metaphors cascading over each other in just the kind of headlong language that we would expect from the big fisherman. And it is especially fascinating that it is Peter, of

all the apostles, who uses this word 'stone' as a description
of a Christian. When Peter was first brought to Jesus by his
brother Andrew, we are told that 'Jesus looked at him and
said, "So you are Simon the son of John? You shall be
called Cephas" (which means Peter)' (John 1.42). There is a
delicate play on words here. The name Peter is normally
the word *petros* in Greek, and means a stone, capable of
being easily picked up, and thrown away. But the word used
by Jesus – 'Cephas' was in the Aramaic language, and means
a 'rock' (*petra* in Greek), something fixed and immovable.
In that prophetic moment, Jesus looked not into Peter's
face, but into his heart and into his future. The word
translated 'looked' means much more than a casual glance;
it speaks of looking into a man, not merely looking him
over. And when Jesus had looked at Peter with divine
insight, he said to him '. . . you are . . . you shall be . . .'.
Jesus saw Peter as he was, and as he was going to be. He
saw a blundering, impetuous, unstable fisherman; but he
foresaw Peter as a solid rock in the Christian faith. On that
momentous day, Jesus not only gave Peter a new name, but
a new character.

This is not the only place where we find this kind of thing
in the Bible. In the early part of the Old Testament, God
says to Abram: 'No longer shall your name be Abram, but
your name shall be Abraham; for I have made you the
father of a multitude of nations' (Genesis 17.5). Later, we
have Jacob's remarkable all-night encounter with a heavenly
visitor, which ended with him being told 'Your name shall
no more be called Jacob, but Israel, for you have striven
with God and with men, and have prevailed' (Genesis
32.28). In both of these cases, as with Peter, a change of
name coincided with a change of nature, a change of
dimension and a change of life's direction. A transformation
was effected. The person involved entered a new world from
that moment on.

So it is with the Christian. Notice that Peter describes
Christians as 'living stones'. In the Authorised Version the
adjective is translated 'lively', but that is both grammatically
and factually deceptive. All Christians are alive in Christ,

but not all are lively! There is a world of difference between the two, just as there is between an Olympic athlete at the peak of his form and someone who has been lying in bed for years with a wasting disease. Both are alive, but only one is lively. There are many Christians who ought to be scaling the mountaintops of spiritual experience, but instead are limping along in the valleys of doubt and defeat.

Nevertheless, when a person is converted, a transformation takes place. This is described in many ways in the Bible, but never more dramatically than when we are told that at conversion a person who was spiritually dead is given new life. Jesus said that the Christian 'has passed from death to life' (John 5.24). John says 'He who has the Son has life; he who has not the Son of God has not life' (1 John 5.12). We came across this same truth in an earlier study, but we need to underline it again and again. Only by understanding it will we get a biblical picture both of man's true state outside of Christ, and of the greatness and glory of our salvation.

Michelangelo was once working on a huge piece of rock when somebody asked him what he was doing. The rock seemed to have no shape or significance at all to the casual onlooker. Turning to his questioner, Michelangelo replied, 'I am releasing the angel that is imprisoned in this marble'. What a transformation there would be when the master's work was finished! Yet this does not begin to compare with what happens when a person becomes a Christian – because there is no angel in our human marble to be released in the first place! All the 'divine spark' theories, teaching as they do that every man is born with some small deposit of spiritual life that needs only to be cultivated, nurtured or developed are so much unbiblical nonsense. Even David, one of the greatest men who ever lived, says 'Behold, I was brought forth in iniquity, and in sin did my mother conceive me' (Psalm 51.5). The Apostle Paul identifies himself with us all when he says that '. . . we were by nature children of wrath like the rest of mankind' (Ephesians 2.3). When a person becomes a Christian, it is not because God applies a dose of heavenly hormones to our celestial embryo, but because in a miracle beyond our understanding he transforms us from being shapeless, useless, inanimate pieces of human rock into what Peter graphically calls 'living stones'. This is the first truth to emerge from our study – the transformation that is effected.

2. *THE INTEGRATION THAT IS REQUIRED.*

Having described Christians as 'living stones', Peter goes on to say 'be yourselves built into a spiritual house'. Notice the order. First we become living stones, then we are to be built into a spiritual house. As Alan Stibbs says 'The phrase . . . implies that men enter the Church by coming to Christ, not that they become joined to Christ by entering the Church'. Notice, too, that the statements are alongside each other. There is nothing in the text between the phrase about becoming living stones and the phrase about being built into a spiritual house, and the lesson is surely obvious: Peter is saying 'As soon as you become a Christian, get integrated. Don't lie around as solitary stones on the world's building sites. Become part of the building'. This is the integration that is required.

One of the current social fads is what we could call 'The Dropout Philosophy'. People are dropping out of society, dropping out of work, dropping out of school, dropping out of home, dropping out of their responsibilities to their fellow-men. In the words of the show, their philosophy is 'Stop the world, I want to get off'. Now I sympathise with people who say 'The whole world has gone mad. We've lost our sense of direction. This isn't the way things ought to be'. I am inclined to agree with Vance Havner when he says 'Civilization is like an ape playing with matches in a room full of dynamite'! But I cannot agree that 'dropping out' is the answer. If things are wrong, let us seek to put them right. If men are going the wrong way, let us show them the right way. If society is mad, let us try to inject some sanity into it.

But these things are not only true in the world; they are also happening in the church. Some folk, and especially

52

young people who have professed conversion in very informal circumstances or in situations outside normal church activities, are opting out of the whole traditional church set-up. In a restless urge to change things, or to get things done, they are trying to bypass the traditional structures and organization of the church and to 'go it alone'. They are turning their backs on the normally accepted church situation and 'doing their own thing'. What can we say about this kind of situation? First, we must be careful not to issue a blanket condemnation of all who do not associate themselves with the ecclesiastical status quo. We have to recognize that in some areas there is no live church for miles. In other places, the churches may be icily unwelcoming to a newcomer who bursts on the scene with what seems like irreverent enthusiasm: the kind of place described by a friend of mine when he said 'It was so cold, I could have skated down the aisle!' Again, there are young couples who live on housing estates too far removed from an evangelical church to make attendance there a reasonable possibility. In these cases, who will lift the first stone to throw at those who, having prayed carefully about the situation in the spirit of James 1.5, begin to conduct Sunday worship in a home, or join with others to meet in a very 'unestablished' way in some 'secular' building? Few things excite me more than modern stories of thriving churches which began in exactly this kind of way.

But the one thing that must be assiduously avoided is Christian *isolationism*, carrying the drop-out philosophy into our Christian experience. The Bible speaks not of dropping out, but of being 'built into a spiritual house'. The writer to the Hebrews is quite specific on this point, when he tells us 'to stir up one another to love and good works, *not neglecting to meet together, as is the habit of some*' (Hebrews 10.25).

Of course the church is far from perfect. Of course it makes mistakes. Of course it has its anachronisms. inconsistencies and hypocrisies. But you will not change those by leaving the church, refusing to meet with other Christians and setting up shop on your own!

A thousand bricks lying around on a building site are of little value. Nobody doubts that they are bricks, but their potential is not realised until they are cemented together with other bricks, and built into something that can give protection, comfort, storage, or a place in which work can be done. Only as part of a building with order, shape and purpose is a brick of real value. In his book *Total Christianity*, Frank Colquhoun says 'As far as the New Testament is concerned, there is no such thing as a churchless Christianity. The church is not a burdensome appendage to the Christian religion; it *is* the Christian religion in its organised form and its outward manifestation'.

No Christian can forward the Kingdom of God better by standing aloof from other Christians like a solitary brick on a building site. Get involved in your local church! Get involved in its programme, its ministry, its prayer life, its burdens, its responsibilities, and its fellowship. Only then will you get involved in its blessings! Only then will you be fulfilling in practical terms the thrust of what Peter is saying in this verse – 'be yourselves built into a spiritual house'.

3. *THE IDENTIFICATION THAT IS SUGGESTED.*

So far, our study has centred entirely on the fact that *Christians* are described as 'living stones'. But in verse 4 of 1 Peter 2 you will see that *Christ* is described as 'that living stone', and in verse 6 that he is described as 'a stone, a cornerstone chosen and precious . . .'. This simple word 'stone' is one of the great biblical definitions not only of Christians but also of the Lord Jesus Christ. Peter is quoting from Isaiah 28.16, where we read 'Behold, I am laying in Zion for a foundation a stone, a tested stone, a precious cornerstone, of a sure foundation', and from Psalm 118.22 where the writer, prophesying the rejection of Christ, says that 'The stone which the builders rejected has become the head of the corner'.

Of the many truths that flow from the statement that Jesus is 'a stone' let us concentrate on just one, that fits perfectly into our present picture. In verses 4 and 6, Jesus is called a stone; in between, in verse 5, Christians are called stones. To put it very simply, the Christians are identified with Christ. I remember leading a house party in Norway on one occasion, on which about seventy of us were having a marvellous time, exploring God's world and God's word. One day it rained so hard, and for so long, that we were 'confined to barracks' (a rather nice hotel!). After the inevitable postcards had been written, people gathered around in informal groups to pass the time away. Some played table games, others read books or chatted. But one group decided to exercise their minds in another way. They took a large sheet of paper, wrote a word at the top of it, and then spent several hours seeing how many other words they could make, using only the letters of their original word. If I remember correctly, they ended with over 200. And the word with which they began? – 'identification'. It was amazing what they made from that one word; and it is wonderful what we can get out of the biblical doctrine that the Christian is identified with Christ.

For instance, at the end of Colossians 2 and the beginning of Colossians 3, we find these four phrases: '. . . *with Christ* you died. . . .' (2.20); '. . . you have been raised *with Christ*' (3.1); '. . . your life is hid *with Christ* in God' (3.3); and 'When Christ who is our life appears, then you also will appear *with him* in glory' (3.4). The Christian is identified with Christ in his rejection, in his resurrection, in his reign and in his return. To put it the other way around, everything that Jesus was and is, everything that Jesus did and does, is linked in with the life of every Christian. The life, death, resurrection, reign and return of Christ are for the benefit and blessing of his people. Christ was rejected by the world, and so is the Christian. Christ rose from the dead, and we too have been raised to newness of life. Christ reigns in glory, and by the means of grace we can lay hold of his reigning power to triumph in all our earthly circumstances. Christ will return to the earth in majesty and great glory, and we shall be taken to be with him for ever. That is identification!

Yet this great truth about the Christian's identification

with Christ carries with it the obvious responsibility to live in such a way that people can recognise our identification in practical terms. Somebody once put it like this: 'If you were arrested on a charge of being a Christian, would there be enough evidence to convict you?' Now there is a question! Imagine yourself in a court of law, charged with being a Christian, a follower of Christ. Think of the people who would be called to give evidence: your husband or wife; your parents or children; your boy friend or girl friend; your boss or your employees; your fellow students; the members of your sports club; the minister of your church. The list is endless – and the possibilities frightening! When they had all given their evidence of what they had seen of your life, would an honest judge convict you? I am afraid that some Christians would be acquitted, and given leave to prosecute the prosecution!

The other obvious point about identification is that we should never be ashamed of being identified with Christ. Some people are perfectly happy about being identified with a particular church or denomination, or theological school of thought, but somehow they feel embarrassed at being identified in a personal way with Christ. Yet our identification is essentially with *him*, and not primarily an organisation. A Christian was once asked 'Don't you belong to the Methodist Church?' He replied 'No, I am a member of the Methodist Church. I belong to Jesus Christ'. No Christian should be ashamed of declaring his allegiance to Christ. To say with Peter under pressure, 'I do not know the man' (Matthew 26.72), even when we say it by our silence, is an act of shameful betrayal. I remember seeing a Muslim take out his prayer mat in the middle of Athens Airport and, apparently oblivious of the hundreds of the other passengers thronging that sophisticated, commercial, secular building, go through his routine of prayer and worship, bowing in the direction of Mecca, his feet bare, his forehead touching the ground. Now I am not suggesting that Christians should occasionally have their Quiet Times in the middle of the Departure Lounge at Heathrow! – but I must say that that unenlightened man spoke deeply to my heart about my willingness to be openly identified with my Lord and Saviour in today's world.

4. *THE OBLATIONS THAT ARE DESIRED.*

Having spoken of Christians as living stones, and urged them to become integrated into the spiritual house of the Christian church, Peter goes on to say that this is in order 'to be a holy priesthood, to offer spiritual sacrifices acceptable to God through Jesus Christ'. In his typically breathless style, he runs one idea into another with bewildering speed. He speaks of Christians as stones, sees them as a building, and at the same time says that they are priests and should be offering sacrifices! In the natural world, there is a vast difference between the building and the people who occupy it, but the Bible is so rich and diverse in its descriptions of Christians that Peter can see us as both. Christians not only form the building, they do so in order to carry out the purpose for which the building is erected. And that purpose, says Peter, is 'to offer spiritual sacrifices acceptable to God through Jesus Christ'.

In the Old Testament, sacrifices were an important part of worship. A special building was set aside for the purpose. Certain people were carefully selected to perform the sacred duties of priests on behalf of the others. Specific animals were taken and sacrificed according to minutely detailed regulations. This is the background of Peter's illustrations, which is contrasted with the position that now exists under the New Covenant. The new emphasis is not on a building, but on the people. *They* form the church. Then, the sacrifices are not to be offered by a select few, but by all, for every Christian is a priest. And finally, the offerings are not animals, but what Peter calls 'spiritual sacrifices'. These are the oblations that God desires.

But what are these 'spiritual sacrifices'? It would be easy to invent a neatly parcelled list of things that would be 'acceptable to God' in our lives, but let us keep precisely to the Bible, and list those things specifically mentioned as being spiritual sacrifices that are pleasing to him.

Firstly, there is sorrow for sin.

In his great penitential Psalm, David says *'The sacrifice acceptable to God* is a broken spirit; a broken and contrite heart, O God, thou wilt not despise' (Psalm 51.17). When the Bible describes Jesus as 'a man of sorrows, and acquainted with grief' (Isaiah 53.3) it is pointing to the weight of our sin, and when we are conscious of unforgiven sin in our lives we, too, should know the stab of sorrow and shame. When the Holy Spirit reveals something in our lives that grieves him, runs contrary to God's law, shows us as being disobedient to his will, we should know what it is to have broken and contrite hearts. Can you remember when you last shed a tear because of sin in your life? Can you remember when last you were genuinely ashamed or brokenhearted because of your behaviour, your language, your pride, your envy, your greed, your coldness of heart, the meanness of your worship, your reluctance to witness for Christ, or any other failure in your life? It is sad when a Christian forgets how to cry over his sin.

Secondly, there is the ministry of money.

In his letter to the Philippians, Paul thanks them for certain gifts that they had made towards his ministry, and goes on – '. . . I am filled, having received from Epaphroditus the gifts you sent, a fragrant offering, *a sacrifice acceptable and pleasing to God'*. When we speak about sacrificial giving, we are usually thinking about the amount of the gift, or its cost to the giver. But Paul is speaking about the spirit in which the gift was given, and its acceptability in the sight of God. To sense whether our giving is a sacrifice 'acceptable and pleasing to God', we must assess it not merely in terms of amount, but of the spirit of the gift, of our willingness to give. Robert Rodenmayer has said that there are three kinds of giving: grudge giving, duty giving and thanksgiving. Grudge giving says 'I have to'; duty giving says 'I ought to'; thanksgiving says 'I want to'. Which is the closest to describing the spirit of your giving to Christian work?

A boy was once given a 50p piece and a 10p piece by his father, and told to put into the offering plate at church that day whichever coin he felt was right in the light of what the Bible taught about giving. After the service, the boy returned the 50p piece to his father. Naturally disappointed, he asked the little fellow why he felt it right to give the smaller amount. 'Because', said junior, 'the Bible says "God loves a cheerful giver" and I was much more cheerful giving 10p than I would have been giving 50p'! I think he missed the point somewhere! Interestingly enough, the word 'cheerful' in 2 Corinthians 9.7 is the Greek word *hilaros*, from which we get our English word 'hilarious'. Generous giving to the Lord should be the constant delight of every Christian. Does this say anything about the spirit in which you exercise the ministry of giving? Do you give in a way that makes your gift 'a fragrant offering, a sacrifice acceptable and pleasing to God'?

Thirdly, there is praise and thanksgiving.

In Hebrews 13.15 we read this – 'Through him then let us continually offer up *a sacrifice of praise to God*, that is, the fruit of lips that acknowledge his Name'. I am convinced that this is often a missing spirit today. Back in the sixteenth century, George Herbert penned this prayer: 'O Thou who hast given us so much, mercifully grant us one thing more, a grateful heart'. We need to pray that kind of prayer often! Paul says that one of the marks of the Spirit-filled man is that he is 'always and for everything giving thanks in the Name of our Lord Jesus Christ to God the Father' (Ephesians 5.20). He tells the Thessalonians to 'give thanks in all circumstances; for this is the will of God in Christ Jesus for you' (1 Thessalonians 5.18). Yet this is far from easy. It is easy to give thanks to God when everything is going well, when the sky is blue and the sea is calm; when everything is peaceful at home, and prosperous at work, when our health is good, and when the Lord is obviously blessing our Christian service. But what happens when difficulties arise, and problems multiply, and the pressures on us mount? Is it not true that thanksgiving is one of the first things to disappear? Preaching on the text 'But the fruit of the spirit is joy. . . .' C. H. Spurgeon once said: 'Brethren, if we ever become perfect in heart, we shall joy

59

in all the divine will, whatever it may bring us. I am trying, if I can, to find a joy in rheumatism, but I cannot get up to it yet. I have found a joy when it is over – I can reach that length – and I can and do bless God for any good result that may come of it; but when the pain is on me, it is difficult to be joyous about it, and so I conclude that my sanctification is very incomplete, and my conformity to the divine will is sadly imperfect'. There spoke an honest man! Let us continually ask God for a grateful heart, whatever he allows or directs to come into our lives.

Fourthly, there is doing good by sharing.

In the very next verse, the writer to the Hebrews says: 'Do not neglect to do good and to share what you have, *for such sacrifices are pleasing to God*' (Hebrews 13.16). When some people speak about a 'do-gooder' today they mean it in an almost derisory way. They have in mind a rather spineless, characterless individual, shuffling around helping lame dogs over stiles; or they think of some tweedy Amazon rattling a collection box in the High Street. But in the Bible a 'do-gooder' is invested with all the dignity of deity, for it is said of the Lord Jesus himself that he 'went about doing good' (Acts 10.38). Nobody need be ashamed of a spirit which draws them to invest their time and talents in helping their fellow men, and sharing with them the good things the Lord has given them. The 'good things' that can be shared in the spirit of our verse in Hebrews are endless. Some commentators think that the writer has the gospel in mind, but in my view his concern is with things much more down-to-earth. The couple with room to spare can offer the freedom of their home to a student looking for digs; the comparatively well-to-do businessman has a better opportunity to give than others; the tradesman can occasionally make his particular goods or services available freely or cheaply to people in genuine need; the housewife with grown-up children off her hands can use her new free time to help the sick, the elderly, the handicapped or the over-stressed. In a nutshell, Christians should be the finest neighbours people could have, and the most generous, open-hearted members of the social circles in which they move. To expand the issue to wider horizons of need which the Christian should help to meet would be to run out of space to mention them – but we could begin with the 400,000,000 people who will go to bed hungry tonight!

The Apostle is quite explicit on the issue: 'So then, as we have opportunity, let us do good to all men, and especially to those who are of the household of faith' (Galatians 6.10). The writer to the Hebrews brings in the warming assurance that the sharing of our goods and gifts with others is something 'pleasing to God'. It is his divinely-ordained way of carrying out his loving and merciful purposes in the world today.

There is a well-known story of a London church badly damaged during an air-raid in World War II. In restoring it for worship, it was found that a statue of Christ had been shattered in pieces. Somebody carefully put it together again, but found that both hands were missing. It stayed like that, looking not only incomplete but pointless, until somebody put underneath it a card with these words: 'Christ has no hands but our hands to do his work today'. Those twelve words said it all!

Chapter 6

A Soldier

Consider these two pictures: first, a group of men, women and children walking slowly through a country churchyard on a Sunday morning, with the sun shining, and the air filled with the mingled melodies of church bells and birdsong; secondly, a blood-drenched battlefield, with a hopelessly outnumbered group of infantrymen completely surrounded by a ruthless and hideous enemy bent on massacre.

It would be difficult to imagine two more totally different

pictures, yet when we open the pages of the Bible, we find that they synchronise in the truth that a Christian is a soldier. If the only books in the Bible were Paul's letters to Timothy, there could be no difficulty in discovering that. He writes 'This charge I commit to you, Timothy, my son, in accordance with the prophetic utterances which pointed to you, that inspired by them you may wage the good warfare' (1 Timothy 1.18). Towards the end of the same letter he urged him to 'Fight the good fight of faith . . .' (1 Timothy 6.12). Near the beginning of his next letter to him he encourages him to 'Take your share of suffering as a good soldier of Christ Jesus' (2 Timothy 2.3).

The picture of the Christian as a soldier, and of the church as an army, has been the inspiration of many of our best-known hymns, such as 'Onward Christian soldiers', 'Fight the good fight', 'Sound the battle-cry', 'Soldiers of Christ, arise', and many others. In the service of Holy Communion laid down in the Book of Common Prayer there is a point where the Minister has an opportunity to indicate special items for prayer. These may be international, social, local church situations, matters concerning individual people in the church, and so on. But whatever these 'biddings' may be, he always ends them with the words 'And let us pray for the whole state of Christ's Church militant here on earth'. Our hymn-books and our church manuals combine to take up this great biblical theme: a Christian is a soldier. In this chapter, we are going to look at three aspects of this truth.

1. THE CHRISTIAN SOLDIER'S OPPOSITION.

Corrie Ten Boom has said that 'The first step on the way to victory is to recognise the enemy', and that is certainly true in the realm of Christian warfare. As we consider the nature of the opposition faced by the Christian soldier, let us begin at the real heart of the matter.

Firstly, it is diabolical.

In other words, it is satanic; it is led, masterminded and planned by the devil, and carried out by him and the unseen hosts of evil at his disposal. Now for some people, a statement like that belongs to the realm of fantasy. They do not believe that there is such a person or power as the devil. A survey carried out in Britain in 1969 revealed that only 21% of the population believed in his existence. Dr. Charles Malik, former President of the United Nations General Assembly, was right when he declared that we have lost the sense of the eternal battle raging between Christ and the devil. No Christian should make that mistake. The Bible describes the devil as a living person, and the implacable enemy of God and the Christian. Paul calls him 'the god of this world' (2 Corinthians 4.4) and 'the prince of the power of the air' (Ephesians 2.2). Jesus refers to him as 'the ruler of this world' (John 14.30). He likens him to a 'strong man, fully armed' (Luke 11.21), and describes him both as 'a murderer from the beginning' and as 'a liar and the father of lies' (John 8.44). The Apostle John names him 'the angel of the bottomless pit' (Revelation 9.11), while Peter warns his readers of him by saying that 'Your adversary the devil prowls around like a roaring lion, seeking someone to devour' (1 Peter 5.8).

The cartoonist's caricature of the devil as a red-faced old man, with pointed ears, a toasting-fork in his hand and his tail sticking out of his trousers is no more than that – a caricature. The Bible declares him to be a living super-power, an evil genius who is unspeakably cruel, incredibly cunning and powerful beyond all human imagination. You have only to look at his track record in the Bible to see that. When Adam and Eve were lured into sin, it was the devil's deadly work; when Job was tempted to turn his back on God, it was as a result of the devil's activities; when Judas Iscariot betrayed Jesus to the authorities at Jerusalem we are told that 'Satan entered into him' (John 13.27); when Paul explains to the Christians at Thessalonica why he had not been able to carry out his evangelistic plans he said plainly 'Satan hindered us' (1 Thessalonians 2.18). These people all tell the same story: 'The devil tempted me'; 'The devil forced me into it'; 'The devil dragged me down'; 'The devil foiled my plans'.

There is no area of our lives that is safe from him, no

63

avenue of approach that is not open to him, and no stage in our lives when we are inaccessible to him. He attacks along all the basic fronts of our lives and personality.

He attacks physically.

Paul says that his 'thorn in the flesh' (nobody seems clear as to the precise nature of this, but it is generally agreed that it was some kind of physical trouble) was 'a messenger of Satan, to harass me. . . .' (2 Corinthians 12.7). The crippled woman in Luke 13 was said by Jesus to be someone 'whom Satan bound for eighteen years' (Luke 13.16). Not all physical illness is the direct work of the devil, but it is obvious from these verses that this is a realm in which he has scope and power to operate.

He attacks mentally.

Paul tells the Christians at Corinth that 'the god of this world has blinded the minds of the unbelievers' (2 Corinthians 4.4) and later on in the same letter confesses 'I am afraid that as the serpent deceived Eve by his cunning, your thoughts will be led astray from a sincere and pure devotion to Christ' (2 Corinthians 11.3). As 'a liar and the father of lies', the devil twists, warps, bends and pollutes the truth. He operates in the realm of the mind, the psyche, the understanding.

Then, obviously, *he attacks spiritually.*

When Ananias and his wife deceived the early church over the selling price of their land, Peter challenged him 'Ananias, why has Satan filled your heart to lie to the Holy Spirit and to keep back part of the proceeds of the land?' (Acts 5.3). He operates in the realm of the heart, the will, the conscience, the desire.

Here, then, is the first thing we must recognise about the opposition we face as Christians. It is diabolical. The Christian life is not a sanctified pop festival. It is a fierce battle against 'the devil and all his works'.

Secondly, it is spiritual.

This follows from the fact that our opponent the devil is a spiritual and not a physical being. Paul puts it like this in Ephesians 6.12: 'For we are not contending against flesh and blood, but against the principalities, against the powers, against the world rulers of this present darkness, against the spiritual hosts of wickedness in the heavenly places'. The opposition the Christian soldier faces is not basically outward and physical, but inward and spiritual. It does have outward, physical and visible manifestations, of course, for example in the area of materialism and sex. But these only reflect something inward and spiritual. The conflicts and issues of life are matters of the mind, the will, the conscience, the heart and the spirit.

Jesus brings this out very clearly when he says: 'Do you not see that whatever goes into a man from outside cannot defile him, since it enters, not into his heart but into his stomach, and so passes on? (Thus he declared all foods clean). And he said "What comes out from a man is what defiles a man. For from within, out of the heart of man, come evil thoughts, fornication, theft, murder, adultery, coveting, wickedness, deceit, licentiousness, envy, slander, pride, foolishness. All these evil things come from within, and they defile a man" ' (Mark 7.18–23).

Nothing could be clearer! The Christian soldier's battle is spiritual, not physical. If you could shut yourself away from all outward temptation, you would still find yourself involved in a spiritual warfare. The battlefield is not on our eyeballs, or on the surface of our skin, but in the treacherous depths of our hearts. The opposition is spiritual!

Thirdly, it is personal.

This is obvious, but let us make the point. While taking part in a conference in West Germany, I had a meal with a German and a Dutchman. Both Christians, they began to reminisce about the Second World War. It transpired that they were fighting (on opposite sides) in the same area of northern Europe at the same time. As they probed deeper, they came to the conclusion that on one particular day they had both been a matter of yards from each other during several hours of hand-to-hand fighting for one particular village. During that time they had been doing their utmost to kill each other – yet their opposition to each other was in no way personal. They did not know each other. The battle they were fighting was one of political and nationalistic forces. It was a battle of ideologies, not of personalities.

Exactly the opposite is true in the Christian warfare. It is personal. Our sin is personal, our salvation is personal – and the battle we fight is personal. When there were only two people on earth, the devil fought them one at a time. So today, with a detailed dossier on our circumstances, our background, our temperament and our weaknesses, he tempts, attacks and fights us as individuals. One has only to read the experiences of New Testament Christians to see that these men were singled out for attack in order that the devil's deadly work might be done.

This truth brings with it a very clear lesson. You cannot escape in the crowd, or shelter under the umbrella of the church, or register as a conscientious objector in today's spiritual warfare. Every Christian is a soldier. Every Christian is in the battle. Every Christian faces diabolical, spiritual and personal opposition. And, as Paul puts it, at the end of the day 'each one of us shall give account of himself to God' (Romans 14.12).

2. THE CHRISTIAN SOLDIER'S OBJECTIVES.

Having seen something of the opposition we face as Christians in today's world, what should our objectives be? I remember Major W. F. Batt telling me 'Maintenance of the objective was the first rule of war I was ever taught'. Whatever his circumstances, a soldier must remember the object of the exercise in which he is engaged, always keep it in the front of his thinking, straining every sinew to fulfil it to the best of his ability, regardless of the cost to himself. Listen to an American serviceman describing a Japanese *kamikaze*, or suicide bomber attack on his ship. 'We saw him coming out of the sun, heading for our ship. We tried desperately to stop him, but he got through our flak and struck the deck and bounced and came to a stop. The bomb was a dud. We opened the cockpit and found a 15-year old Japanese boy, still alive, chained inside.'

That pilot escaped because the bomb his plane was carrying was faulty: but he was so committed to his cause

66

that he was prepared to maintain his objective even at the cost of his own life.

In ways that may be less dramatic, but should be no less positive, the Christian soldier is called upon to discipline himself to maintain life's spiritual objectives. What are they?

Firstly, the enemy's withdrawal.

Two friends who share my deep interest in Czechoslovakia once told me of their reaction when the Warsaw Pact countries invaded it in 1968. 'This is God's country,' they told me, 'and the devil has taken it over. We are going to do everything we can to push him back by taking the gospel there.' Their statement was idealistic, dramatic, and, of course, not strictly true. Czechoslovakia is no more God's country than are the Warsaw Pact countries. Nor would the withdrawal of all Communist influence automatically produce a Christian revival in the country. But I understood what they meant, and their vivid language illustrates the objective that ought to be firmly in the heart of every Christian. The prophet Isaiah says 'But now thus says the Lord, he who created you, O Jacob, he who formed you, O Israel: "Fear not, for I have redeemed you; I have called you by name, you are mine. . . ." ' (Isaiah 43.1). As we face the devil's attacks we need to keep this firmly in mind. God has created and redeemed us, and calls us his own. Everything we are and have belongs to him. The devil has no right to your eyes, your feet, your hands, your body, your mind, your time, or your talents. All of these belong to *God*. They are exclusively *his*! The Christian's philosophy of battle ought therefore to include a determination to repel every attempt of the devil to occupy God's territory.

But let us be careful here, and not fall into a subtle trap. We will never succeed in destroying the devil. Nor can we get rid of him for the rest of our lives. There is no such thing in genuine Christian experience as a once-for-all dramatic crisis that gets rid of the process of fighting the devil throughout our lives. When Jesus was in the wilderness, he faced and repelled three attacks by the devil. We then read that 'when the devil had ended every temptation, he departed from him *until an opportune time*' (Luke 4.13).

This was neither the first nor the last time that Jesus faced temptation and the attacks of the enemy. He continued to be attacked and tempted throughout his life. The writer to the Hebrews describes Jesus as 'One who has been tempted in every way, just as we are . . .' (Hebrews 4.15 New International Version). The temptation in the wilderness was not a once-for-all crisis, it was merely a highlight in a life-long battle.

We, too, face a life-long battle. The devil will attack us repeatedly. Yet as often as he attacks, so often are we to aim at his withdrawal. By prayer, faith, discipline, Christian fellowship, and the Word of God we are to aim at the fulfilment of the promise given to us in the Bible: 'Submit yourselves therefore to God. Resist the devil and he will flee from you' (James 4.7). The enemy's withdrawal is one clear objective the Christian must have.

Secondly, the Lord's approval.

This is how Paul puts it in writing to Timothy: 'No soldier on service gets entangled in civilian pursuits, since his aim is *to satisfy the one who enlisted him*' (2 Timothy 2.4). The life of Jesus personified that principle. He says to those arguing about his mission in the world that as the Son of Man he was acting under his heavenly Father's authority, and 'I always do *what is pleasing to him*' (John 8.29). This theme runs right through the Bible. Writing to Christians in Greece about the ministry of evangelism, Paul says that his aim was 'not to please men, but *to please God* who tests our hearts' (1 Thessalonians 2.4). Moving on to encourage them to live godly lives, he gives them this motive: 'Finally, breathren, we beseech and exhort you in the Lord Jesus, that as you learned from us how you ought to live and *to please God*, just as you are doing, you do so more and more' (1 Thessalonians 4.1). The writer of the Epistle to the Hebrews says of Enoch that 'before he was taken, he was commended as one *who pleased God*' (Hebrews 11.5 New International Version). Paul encourages the Colossians to 'lead a life worthy of the Lord, *fully pleasing to him*' (Colossians 1.10). And finally John tells of consistent answers to prayer 'because we keep his commandments *and do what pleases him*' (1 John 3.22).

All of this teaches us an important truth about living the Christian life, and that is that being a Christian is not a matter of rules and regulations, quotas and ratios, mathematics and percentages. Nowhere are we told to aim at a certain 'percentage of purity'. Basically, the Christian life is one of relationship with the Lord. It is not a matter of passing some clinical examination, but of seeking in all things to be 'fully pleasing to him'.

I remember, as a young Christian, discussing with a speaker from England whether we beginners in the faith ought to study for some kind of theological examination, and perhaps even aim at a degree. Did he think this was a good idea? 'Yes I do,' he smiled, 'I think you ought all to aim for the A.U.G.' Well, that stumped us! We had heard of the B.A., the M.A., the Dip.Th., and so on, but we had never heard of the A.U.G. Where could we find out about it? 'In 2 Timothy 2.15,' was his simple reply. Turning it up, we found this: 'Study to shew thyself *approved unto God. . . .*' (2 Timothy 2.15 AV). The message was loud and clear! Every Christian ought to have it as a settled aim in life that he will always seek God's approval on all that he does, constantly regulating and adjusting his life according to the leading of the Holy Spirit and the teaching of the Word of God.

These, then, are the twin objectives of the Christian soldier, the enemy's withdrawal and the Lord's approval. In other words, we should always aim to be looking at the Lord's face and the devil's back. Happy the Christian who is familiar with those two views!

3. *THE CHRISTIAN SOLDIER'S OPTIMISM.*

During World War I, Marshal Foch sent this famous message to General Joffre: 'My right is broken, my left is shattered, my centre is in retreat. The situation is excellent; let us attack!' That must have sounded like super-optimism to the soldiers concerned, and perhaps it may sound strange to speak of the Christian soldier's optimism in the light of all we have studied about the devil's tremendous power, and the great demands made upon us to seek the enemy's withdrawal and the Lord's approval. Yet the Christian soldier can enter every day of his spiritual warfare with genuine optimism, with a happy heart, and with confidence that he can emerge victorious, and we will close this study by looking at three reasons for this.

Firstly, because God's provisions are available.

The classic biblical passage on Christian warfare is in Ephesians 6, where Paul speaks not only about the Christian's enemies but also lists the equipment available to him for the contest. With no space for detailed comment, let us just remind ourselves of Paul's words as paraphrased by Kenneth Taylor in The Living Bible: 'So use every piece of God's armour to resist the enemy whenever he attacks, and when it is all over, you will still be standing up. But to do this, you will need the strong belt of truth and the breastplate of God's approval. Wear shoes that are able to speed you on as you preach the Good News of peace with God. In every battle you will need faith as your shield to stop the fiery arrows aimed at you by Satan. And you will need the helmet of salvation and the sword of the Spirit – which is the Word of God.' Each of these items deserves its own detailed study, but the essential point is that they are all part of God's provision for the Christian soldier – *and because God has provided them, they must be effective.* When a Christian loses a battle, it is always because he has not rightly used the equipment that God has provided for his defence and protection, and for repelling the enemy. If you want to be an effective soldier for Christ – whether or not you get earthly promotion! – study Ephesians 6, and learn how to put your battledress on!

Secondly, because God's promises are accessible.

In the seventeenth century William Gurnall, a Church of England minister, wrote a classic book on Ephesians 6.10–17. In its original form the book ran to 877 pages, but the modern version dashes it off in a mere 603! In what we would now call the foreword to the book – but then called 'The Epistles Dedicatory' – Gurnall wrote, in the quaint language of his time: 'Whet your courage at the throne of grace, from whence all your recruits of soul-strength come. *Send faith oft up the hill of promise*, to see and bring you the certain news of Christ's coming to you, yea, and assured victory with him'. Quaint it may be, but it is right on line. The Christian soldier can fight with confidence because of the many promises that are his in God's Word. Let me remind you of two, one as it were for every day, and one for life's battle as a whole. The first is one we have already quoted, where James says 'Submit yourselves therefore to God. Resist the devil *and he will flee from you*' (James 4.7). That is a promise! As we have seen, he will not flee for ever. He will not leave you unmolested. But God has promised that the devil's attacks *can* be turned back. The second promise is where Paul writes 'I have fought the good fight, I have finished the race, I have kept the faith. Henceforth there is laid up for me the crown of righteousness, which the Lord, the righteous judge, will award me on that Day, and not only to me but also to all who have loved his appearing' (2 Timothy 4.7–8). That is another promise! The day will come when the battle will be ended, the last attack will be over, the last temptation will have died away, the last pressure will have been lifted – and you will stand secure in God's eternal presence wearing what Paul calls 'the crown of righteousness'. How confidently would an athlete run if he knew he was going to win the race? How confidently would a soldier fight if he was certain that his enemy would lie defeated at the end of the day? Every Christian should face the battle of life with the same happy assurance. The war is not easy. We are likely to get hurt, and some of us very badly. But we are all on the winning side!

Thirdly, because God's presence is assured.

Everybody knows the Old Testament story of David and Goliath. When these two stood face to kneecaps in front of the Philistines and the Israelites, any boxing official would have declared it 'No contest'. Goliath was 9′ 9″ tall. He had a coat of armour that weighed twelve stone. The head of his spear tipped the scales at 15 lbs. All David seemed to have was a sling, five stones and a suntan! But when Goliath had

71

finished ranting. David looked at him calmly and said: 'You come to me with a sword and with a spear and with a javelin; but I come to you in the name of the Lord of hosts, the God of the armies of Israel whom you have defied. This day the Lord will deliver you into my hand . . . for the battle is the Lord's, and he will give you into our hand' (1 Samuel 17.45–47).

David was expressing his unflinching faith in one decisive fact – that God was fighting on his side. Anything he would do in the battle would be done not in his strength, but in the power of the living God. No wonder he was confident – and the same confidence, for the same reason, is re-stated throughout the Bible. The Psalmist says '*Through thee* we push down our foes; *through thy name* we tread down our assailants' (Psalm 44.5). Paul writes 'For though we live in the world we are not carrying on a worldly war, for the weapons of our warfare are not worldly but have *divine power* to destroy strongholds' (2 Corinthians 10.3–4). Warning the Romans of the opposition we face, he nevertheless goes on to assert that 'in all these things we are more than conquerors *through him* who loved us' (Romans 8.37). He even dares to tell the Philippians 'I can do all things *in him* who strengthens me' (Philippians 4.13). Here is the open secret of Christian confidence even against the satanic opposition he faces day by day. The Christian soldier is called upon to watch fight, pray, resist, struggle, be disciplined, wrestle, strive; these are his inescapable responsibilities. *But he is never called upon to do so in his own strength.* As Paul says in that passage from Ephesians 6, the Christian is to 'be strong in the Lord and in the strength of his might' (Ephesians 6.10).

In ordinary warfare, the strength of a general lies in that of his troops. In the spiritual warfare, the strength of the troops – the Christians – lies in the power of their General. William Gurnall is 'spot-on' here: 'Take heart therefore, O ye saints, and be strong; your cause is good, God himself espouseth your quarrel, who hath appointed you his own Son, General of the field, called "Captain of our salvation". He shall lead you on with courage, and bring you off with honour. He lived and died for you; he will live and die with you; for mercy and tenderness to his soldiers, none like him. . . . For success insuperable: he never lost a battle even when he lost his life: he won in the field, carrying the spoils thereof, in the triumphant chariot of his ascension, to heaven with him: where he makes an open show of them to the unspeakable joy of saints and angels'.

Praise the Lord! Onward Christian soldiers!

Chapter 6

A Steward

Among the many books in my study, one of the most battered is an old etymological dictionary. Etymology is the study of the origins of words, and I find it fascinating to discover exactly how words we use commonly today came into being. Someone once told me 'Your English language is the richest in the world, because you have taken from Greek, Latin, French, German and so many other languages in order to make your own.' He was probably right – and delving back into an English word's 'family tree' is an absorbing business.

Take the very ordinary word 'steward', for instance. How would you explain it in a simplified dictionary? It is not easy to condense the ideas that come to mind into one small phrase. But let us look at the etymology, and see what we find. The word comes from the Middle English word 'stiward' and the Anglo-Saxon 'sti-weard'. The 'sti' part is a shortened form of the ancient word 'stig' or 'stiga', which was probably a house (the nearest word we have from this root today is the word 'sty'); while the 'weard' part has now become 'ward' (to guard or take care of). Putting all that together, we would have something like 'to take care of a house or property'.

All very fascinating, but does it have anything to do with our present series of studies? Yes, it has, for one of the New Testament definitions of a Christian is that of a steward. But New Testament Greek has its own etymology (which is neither Middle English nor Anglo-Saxon!), and our 'steward' is the word *oikonomos*, which is made up of two separate words. The first, *oikos*, means 'a house', and the second *nemo*, means 'to arrange'. We can therefore see that our English word is an excellent translation of the original. A steward is the arranger, or manager, of a house or property. He is someone appointed to be in charge of an estate, for instance, usually in the absence of the owner. These days a steward can also refer to somebody in charge of a race meeting, or serving drinks behind a bar; but the sense is the same: he is in charge of property belonging to somebody else.

Here endeth the etymological lesson! – but it will all be helpful as we study three aspects of the fact that the Bible calls a Christian a steward.

1. *THE RESPONSIBILITY OF CHRISTIAN STEWARDSHIP.*

It is already obvious that stewardship is a responsible position, whether the property concerned is great or small. In fact, responsibility is the very essence of stewardship. It is almost a synonym for it. We could say that stewardship virtually *means* responsibility. Jesus told a parable which began like this: 'There was a rich man who had a steward, and charges were brought to him that this man was wasting his goods. And he called him and said to him, "What is this that I hear about you? Turn in the account of your stewardship. . . ." ' (Luke 16.1–2). Those opening phrases capture the spirit of stewardship. It involves responsibility. Paul reinforces this point when he lays down the basic qualification for good stewardship: '. . . it is required of stewards that they be found *trustworthy*' (1 Corinthians 4.1). To underline this, let us look at this responsibility a little more closely.

Firstly, it is an individual responsibility.

The Bible puts it like this: 'As each has received a gift, employ it for one another, as good stewards of God's varied grace . . .' (1 Peter 4.10). The first thing to notice from this is that every Christian has received some kind of gift (what the Amplified Bible calls 'a particular spiritual talent'). The Christian who opts out of all service in the world and all responsibility in the church, and who trys to shelter under the excuse that he has nothing to offer, is being nothing short of blasphemous. The Bible says plainly that 'each has received a gift'. Notice that carefully! Beware of escaping the trap of extravagant pride only to fall into the pit of false humility. Let me quote some words from *The Song of the Virgin* by Spiros Zodhiates – '. . . if you're leading a useless life, you're not being humble; you're just plain lazy. . . . Many a man, while seriously believing that he was exercising an acceptable humility, has buried his talents in the earth, hidden his light under a bushel, lived a useless life when he might have been a blessing to many. . . . Our humility serves us falsely when it leads us to shrink from any duty. The plea of unfitness or inability is utterly insufficient to excuse us. . . . Your talent may be very small – so small that it scarcely seems to matter whether you use it or not, so far as its impression on the world or on other lives is concerned. Yet no one can know what is small and what is great in this life, in which every cause starts consequences that reach into eternity.' Does that say anything to you? Does it challenge your lack of involvement in God's work? Does it speak to your laziness, or selfishness, while the world is in such a terrible condition, and the church is crying out for help?

The second thing we see from this verse is that every gift we have is the result of 'God's varied grace'. No talent or ability is of our own making or deserving. Every one is given to us freely by God as an unmerited favour. Writing about stewardship to the Christians at Corinth, Paul asks 'What have you that you did not receive?' (1 Corinthians 4.7) – and then adds 'If then you received it, why do you boast as if it were not a gift?' Do you see the point of his question? Write down on a sheet of paper all the talents, gifts and abilities that you have. Then take a separate sheet and this time write down only those that you have *not* received as a free, unmerited gift from God. At the end of the exercise, your first sheet will be full, and the second empty! Every gift you have is the result of God's grace in your life. Boasting is out!

The third thing to notice is that the gifts Christians have are the result of 'God's *varied* grace'. Not everybody has the same gift or ability or talent. Paul recognises this quite clearly when he writes: 'Are all apostles? Are all prophets? Are all teachers? Do all work miracles? Do all possess gifts of healing? Do all speak with tongues? Do all interpret?' (1 Corinthians 12.29–30). The answer, by inference, is in the negative. Christians vary in their gifts as much as in their temperaments – but all have some gifts, and for the exercise of those gifts they are accountable to God. The famous American statesman Daniel Webster was once asked which was the most important subject that had ever occupied his attention. His reply was 'My personal responsibility'. Christians should capture something of that spirit! Paul says bluntly that '. . . each one of us shall give account of himself to God' (Romans 14.12). The day will come when each of us will have to reveal how we have exercised our individual responsibility.

Secondly, it is an irresistible responsibility.

We cannot escape from it. We cannot shake it off. No Christian has the luxury of being able to say 'I am happy to be a son, delighted to be a saint, and honoured to be a soldier – but I would rather not be a steward'. He does not have that option. He cannot be excused from his responsibility to make use of the gifts God has given him.

Let me illustrate from one simple command given by Jesus to the disciples. Just before his ascension into heaven, he told them of the coming of the Holy Spirit upon them and added, '. . . and you shall be my witnesses in Jerusalem, and in all Judea and Samaria and to the end of the earth' (Acts 1.8). Jesus did not say that they *might* be his witnesses, or that they *could* be if they wished. This was an imperative – 'you *shall*'. They had no option. The only question was whether they would be good witnesses or bad. So today,

76

every Christian in the world is a witness, he is a steward of the fact that he is saved. To put it another way, he is an exhibit, on display to the world. What is more, the world will very largely judge the truth of Christianity by the credibility of the witnesses, the exhibits. Jesus says 'He who is not with me is against me, and he who does not gather with me scatters' (Matthew 12.30). No words could possibly put our responsibility more strongly! Are you with Jesus, or against him? Perhaps you find that question easy to answer. You can point to the day when you received him as your Saviour and Lord; you can state quite categorically that you are on his side. But what about the second part of the statement? Are you gathering with him or scattering? Is your life an influence in drawing others to him, or in driving them from him? Are people more likely to believe the Christian case because of the way you live, or does your life make it more difficult for them to believe? As someone once put it, is your life a Bible or a libel? Privilege and responsibility are two sides of the one coin. To be a steward is a great privilege, but it is also a great responsibility, and one that is both individual and irresistible.

2. THE REALM OF CHRISTIAN STEWARDSHIP

There is a sense in which this section of our study is unnecessary. I remember a young Christian telling her friends what a wonderful difference Christ had made to her life. She spoke about her church life, her new understanding of the Bible, her change of attitude towards her parents, and so on. After listening to her for some time, somebody asked 'But what about the other parts of your life?' Nancy replied 'But there are no other parts. He is the Lord of the whole of my life.' That was a great answer! – and it underlines what we have already seen about stewardship. We are stewards of all of life, of everything we are and have. 'There are no other parts'. Yet that can be so vague that we can escape in generalities. Let us therefore look at some of the areas in which we are held to be stewards.

Firstly, the stewardship of time.

Paul says 'Look carefully then how you walk, not as unwise men but as wise, making the most of the time, because the days are evil' (Ephesians 5.15–16). A tiny Greek lesson will help us here. There are two Greek words translated 'time' in our English Bibles. One is *chronos*, from which we get the word 'chronology'. But the other word is *kairos*, which means a measured period of time, something limited, fixed and definite. It is this second word that we have here. Paul is saying that each Christian must make the most of his particular piece of time – in other words, his own lifetime. The Bible tells us that 'David . . . served the counsel of God in his own generation . . .' (Acts 13.36) – the only one in which he could! That was his *kairos*, his own God-given, fixed, limited period of time.

Notice, too, that Paul says we are to be *'making the most of the time'*. The Greek word used is *exagorazo*, which means 'to buy out'. It comes from the market-place, and is the kind of phrase you might use about somebody buying up the entire stock. For the Christian time is a precious commodity to be used to the full, remembering that the stock is limited.

In the late 1850's, as a boy of ten, Thomas Edison tried to solve the problem of human flight by persuading another lad to take a vast overdose of salts! The experiment was a dismal, and no doubt painful, failure! But by the time Edison was 80 he had taken out over 1000 patents. He won the Nobel Prize for Physics in 1915. He became known as 'the man whose workshop changed the world'. He invented the phonograph and the electric light bulb, and played a major part in the invention and development of the microphone, the telephone and many other scientific instruments. He worked about eighteen hours a day, slept only when he was tired and ate only when he was hungry. This remarkable man once said 'Time is not a commodity that can be stored for future use. It must be invested hour by hour or else it is gone for ever'. Edison's life-style may not be the wisest pattern to follow, but every Christian should see the point of his obvious logic, and carry it into the stewardship of his time. While the world speaks about *spending* time, the

Bible speaks about *buying* it! Are you sure that you are on the right side of the counter?

Secondly, the stewardship of leisure.

The period we spend in leisure is, of course, part of the total time available to us, but it is so often overlooked as part of our stewardship, that I want us to deal with it separately. Somebody suggested to a friend of mine that a Christian should never take a complete holiday, but should always be as busy as possible in active Christian service. Holidays should be spent on evangelistic campaigns, beach missions, youth camps, doing literature work or some other form of evangelism, while his 'day off' should be just as fully used. When my friend suggested that surely a rest was sometimes needed, the other man replied 'Certainly not. Look at the devil, he never takes a rest'. 'And since when', my friend countered, 'should a Christian follow the devil's example?' Collapse of hyper-active Christian!

A wise old preacher once said 'For everything there is a season, and a time for every matter under heaven' (Ecclesiastes 3.1), and without any doubt for the Christian (as for everybody else) that includes a time for sensible, restorative rest, change and recreation. Jesus told the disciples to 'Come away by yourselves to a lonely place, and rest a while' (Mark 6.31) – and it is very significant to notice that he said this at a time when '. . . many were coming and going. . . .'. It was while they were surrounded by people in great physical and spiritual need that Jesus withdrew his disciples for a break, in order to re-charge their batteries.

This question of the use of leisure is difficult to get into perspective in today's world. With the whole pace of life getting faster all the time, people are finding it more and more difficult to use their leisure time wisely, even though the amount becoming available is, at least theoretically, increasing every year. Vance Havner somewhere tells the story of two people who discovered that their home towns were fairly near each other. One of them said 'You know, I used to visit your town once a week back in the horse and buggy days. It took me a day to get there and back, but I enjoyed it. I could do it in half an hour now by car, but I just don't have the time'! When you come to think of it, 'I don't have the time' is a strange phrase to use, because we all have exactly the same amount of time – 24 hours in every day. The all-important thing is how we use it.

Let me apply that to the question of leisure. The Christian should make a specific assessment of his leisure in terms of the total stewardship of his time. To give an obvious example, I do not think that a Christian is investing his leisure time wisely if he spends night after night lolling in front of a television set, using it as chewing gum for the eyes. There is something pathetically sad about the thought of countless people all over the country allowing a one-eyed god to dictate their entire thinking processes for 25 per cent of their waking hours, bathing their minds from seven till eleven in politics and pop, drama and detergents, overkill and underwear. Somebody once calculated that by the time the average American child was fourteen he could expect to have seen 18,000 people killed on television. By the time he left high school he would have seen 350,000 commercials, and all in all he would spend ten years of his life watching television! By any reckoning, that is surely a mite too much: in terms of a Christian's stewardship of time, it is criminal.

If a man's leisure-time exercise consists only of changing channels, it is not only his legs that will become atrophied! – nor will that kind of thing restore the Christian's soul, sharpen his mind, or deepen his discipleship.

Now of course, television is not wrong in itself. It is something that God allowed man to discover and develop, and is therefore capable of being used to enrich his life. Television can be a great educator, not only explicitly through the Open University and schools programmes, but also in the wider areas of current affairs, history, travel, nature and the like. It can also be a marvellous entertainer, in the fields of comedy, sport, music and so on. But for too many Christians it has become a subtle dictator, robbing them of so much, and giving them so little that is really worthwhile and beneficial in return. Here, certainly, is something which – if you will pardon the phrase – must be looked at very carefully! But we must examine the whole

80

question of leisure wisely in the context of our work, our age, our health, and all our other circumstances. To be absurd for a moment, it would be a little less than wise for a ninety-three-year-old Christian who decided that he was not getting enough exercise to join evening classes for all-in wrestling! Equally, a healthy sixteen-year-old who spends all his working hours sitting at a desk is not wise to spend all his off-work times sunk in an armchair reading books. Now I imagine that you fit in somewhere between the two! -- but the principle remains the same. Examine your leisure time as part of your stewardship. Look upon it as something the Lord has given you to enrich your life. Plan it sensibly – and then *enjoy* it! I can promise you that it need not interfere with your sanctification!

Thirdly, the stewardship of money.

This is an obvious area of stewardship and because money is something tangible, it is relatively easy to assess. The whole question of giving is a fascinating subject, but we have space here to do no more than establish a principle and ask a question.

The principle first.

In 1 Chronicles 29 we read of the building of the great temple in Jerusalem, about 1000 BC. King David gave over-all direction to his son Solomon, then charged the people of Israel with the responsibility of raising the vast sum of money needed. In an amazing demonstration of generosity and sacrifice, a sum equalling many millions of pounds was given – without a single lottery or bingo session! 'Then the people rejoiced because these had given willingly, for with a whole heart they had offered freely to the Lord' (1 Chronicles 29.9). Naturally, David shared in their great rejoicing, and immediately offered a prayer of praise and thanksgiving to the Lord for this wonderful response. Notice carefully what he said: '. . . And now we thank thee, our God, and praise thy glorious name. But who am I, and what is my people, that we should be able thus to offer willingly? *For all things come from thee, and of thine own have we given thee*' (1 Chronicles 29.13–14).

Having given millions of pounds to the project, the people

6

had given only what belonged to the Lord in the first place. Let every Christian make a careful note of that! Even if we were to give everything we had, we would have given nothing that was not in the first place God's gift to us. That one biblical principle puts all our giving in its correct perspective. For instance, it applies in the matter of tithing. It seems clear to me from the Scriptures that a Christian should give at least one-tenth of his gross income directly to God's service: but the remainder is not his to do with as he pleases. The principle, remember, is that all of his money belongs to the Lord, and he is as responsible to God for the use of the nine-tenths as for the one-tenth. On that basis, perhaps you should be doing some radical re-thinking about the way in which you use God's money. Maybe you should be asking some questions about the amount you spend on clothing, or records, or food, or sport, or other things. You might even need to look at this matter of tithing again!

Now the question.

Are you giving to the Lord what is right – or what is left? To put the question another way: do you deal with your own needs first, and then give the Lord something from what is left over? Or is God first in the stewardship of your money? A friend of mine who has been in Christian service for many years once said 'Unconsecrated Christian wealth is the greatest hindrance to Christian progress', and I am inclined to agree with him. It hinders progress in the spiritual life of the Christian concerned, because God has promised blessing to the giver; and it hinders progress in Christian work, one cause after another having to withdraw from the field, or cut down its programme because of the lack of funds. Are you part of the problem, or part of the answer?

Fourthly, the stewardship of our special gifts.

At the end of what we could call the parable of the stewardship of life, Jesus establishes a vitally important principle: 'Every one to whom much is given, of him will much be required; and of him to whom men commit much they will demand the more' (Luke 12.48). For you, that can only mean one thing: your responsibility exactly matches the gifts God has given you.

A young man once became blind through illness. He lived, however, to a ripe old age, and just before he died, he said 'I thank thee, Father, for the gift of blindness'. His name? – Louis Braille, inventor of the most widely-used blind reading system in the world. I find that deeply challenging! If he could say that about blindness, what of the person with sight, health, strength, and a host of other gifts? Some have the gift of friendship; some the gift of communication; some the gift of hospitality; some a great ability to organize; some great practical ability; some the gift of administration; some the gift of music; some can type; others have the gift of writing. We could go on ad infinitum – and all of these gifts are needed in the church today.

We need, however, to add a careful rider here. I can remember the time early in my Christian life when I felt that my nine-to-five office job was merely a way of earning money, and that life's *real* work came after office hours, when I was involved in the church, the youth fellowship, island-wide evangelism, and so on. I can now see that that was an enthusiastic error – and by sharing it I hope that others can be prevented from making the same mistake. Believing in the sovereignty of God in your life implies a conviction that he has placed you in your 'secular' job or position, and that he has done so for a specific purpose. You are as important to him there as you are at the Y.P.F., or the church prayer meeting. The ability to work is God-given, and to use that gift honourably and efficiently is valid stewardship and genuine testimony.

But of course what we particularly have in mind here is the use of 'secular' gifts in 'spiritual' settings, and in this area it is vital to grasp one great principle: whatever your particular gift, God can use it for the extension of his kingdom, the building of his church, the blessing of his people, the conversion of sinners, and the glory of his name. What an exhilarating thought! God may not specifically use your *qualifications* (a B.A. degree will not of itself make anyone a better Bible class leader, for instance), but he can always use your gifts to his glory. That being so, Paul's words to Timothy need to be heard loud and clear, and heeded here and now: 'Do not neglect the gift you have . . .' (1 Timothy 4.14). Exercise to the full the stewardship of your special gifts!

Fifthly, the stewardship of the gospel.

Paul writes to the church at Corinth, 'This is how one should regard us, as servants of Christ and stewards of the mysteries of God' (1 Corinthians 4.1), and what was true of Paul in a special way is true for every Christian in a general way. Not every Christian is called to be a preacher, lead a Bible class, be a missionary, or take a position of public leadership in the church – but every Christian is called to share in the evangelization of the world. The gospel has been given to you as a sacred trust. Are you a good steward of what Paul calls 'the mysteries of God'? If every member of your church did as much as you to reach people with the gospel, would your church be building an extension or closing down? Someone has put the challenge like this 'to be "in Christ" is to be involved. You did not choose to be in the business of bringing men to Christ – you chose Christ, and you are in the business. You may shrink from it, fumble it, refuse to do it, but you are never absolved from the fact and responsibility of it'. How good a steward of the Gospel are you?

3. *THE REWARD OF CHRISTIAN STEWARDSHIP.*

Although there are some real difficulties in interpreting the parable of the talents in Matthew 25, one principle stands out very clearly: God will reward Christians in heaven according to their stewardship. So, in the parable, the man who had been given five talents and the man who had been given two talents were both rewarded with their master's 'Well done, good and faithful servant; you have been faithful over little, I will set you over much; enter into the joy of your master' (Matthew 25.21, 23).

Paul takes up exactly the same point when he writes, 'For we must all appear before the judgment seat of Christ, so that each one may receive good or evil, according to what he has done in the body' (2 Corinthians 5.10). There is no question here of a Christian being lost, for the judgement of which Paul is speaking here is one of the Christian's works, 'what he has done'. No steward will be turned out of the household of God, but there will be differences in the rewards they receive and these will not be according to their fame but according to their faithfulness. Stewards will be rewarded not according to the measure of their gift, but their use of it. That being so, surely every Christian should seek to be a wise and trustworthy steward of all that God has given him, living and longing for the day when he will look into the Lord's face and hear his voice saying 'Well done, good and faithful servant . . . enter into the joy of your Master'!

A medical student once took a first class honours degree at Edinburgh University. His friends speculated about his future. Further degrees? Lecturing? A professorship perhaps? To their astonishment, he announced that he was going to the foreign mission field. Stunned that he should apparently throw away such great prospects, they said 'But that's no way to get on in the world'. His reply was simple and unanswerable: '*Which world?*'

To be a good steward in God's eyes is infinitely more important than to be a great success in the world's; and the rewards are beyond comparison!

Chapter 7

A V.I.P.

There is no such person as an ordinary Christian. There are *average* Christians (too many) and *normal* Christians (too few) – but none who can be described as ordinary. Let me explain.

It must surely be obvious that the average Christian's

spiritual standard of living is a long way below the pattern we see in the New Testament. Vance Havner has said that we are so subnormal that if we ever became normal, people would think us abnormal! Even if we cannot put it as cleverly as that, we can sadly agree with his assessment. And the normal Christian? Watchman Nee discusses this at the beginning of his well-known book *The Normal Christian Life*, where he says that his aim is 'to show that it is something very different from the life of the average Christian'. He goes on to show that the normal Christian life is one of godliness, victory, progress, and spiritual health, a life filled with Christ. On that assessment, there are too many average Christians and not enough who are normal.

Nevertheless, I maintain that no Christian is ordinary, and as a biblical starting-point let me take you to Ephesians 2. This chapter has a catalogue of contrasts between what these Christians were before and after conversion. The whole point is made by two little phrases: 'you were *at that time*' (v. 12) and '*but now* in Christ' (v. 13). Paul makes a similar point later, where he says, '*once you were* darkness, *but now you are* light in the Lord . . .' (Ephesians 5.8). In an earlier study we saw the same thing at that first meeting between Jesus and Peter, when Jesus looked at the raw, rugged fisherman and said '. . . you are . . . you shall be . . .'. Things were going to change for Peter, as they do for everyone who becomes a Christian. Returning to Paul, we find him stating the same thing even more specifically when he writes to the Corinthians 'Therefore, if any one is in Christ, he is a new creation; the old has passed away, behold, the new has come' (2 Corinthians 5.17).

What a telling phrase that is! The Christian is not an improvement; he is an innovation. He is a new creation, a different person altogether; and it is in that sense that we can say that there is no such thing as an ordinary Christian. No Christian is 'run of the mill', or 'one of the crowd'. Of course the Christian is in a minority in the world – he always has been – but the important thing to notice is that it is a *select* minority, *and God has made the selection!*

Of the many places in the Bible where this is emphasised,

none is clearer than the following definition of God's people in 1 Peter 2.9: 'But you are a chosen race, a royal priesthood, a holy nation, God's own people, that you may declare the wonderful deeds of him who called you out of darkness into his marvellous light'. Look at those adjectives! – 'chosen', 'royal', 'holy', 'God's own'. Hardly ordinary, are they? Yet they apply to every Christian in the world without exception. Then why do they seem such extraordinary, and extravagant definitions of today's professing Christians? I believe there are two reasons.

Firstly, there are many masquerading as Christians with no genuine experience of Christ and therefore no right to that name. There is a story about a rich American couple on holiday in Florida. On the first day, the husband got into difficulties while swimming, and was dragged ashore by two lifeguards. One of them turned to the man's anxious wife and said 'I think we ought to give him artificial respiration'. With a horrified gasp, the wife snapped 'How dare you give my husband anything artificial. We can afford the real thing!' There are many people in our churches today without the real thing. They have never experienced the new birth – and are therefore incapable of sustaining the new life. They are being kept going by the artificial respiration of religious observance, theological beliefs or acceptable behaviour – but they have no genuine spiritual life.

Secondly, many Christians have failed to grasp the reality of their spiritual position. They have never discovered at any depth what the Bible has to say about their status and significance as Christians. Sometimes over-anxious about the ways in which they may differ from other Christians, sometimes nervously pre-occupied with whether there is some other experience they ought to have, they have failed to realise the status and resources that are already theirs in common with all other Christians. Now there are obviously many ways in which Christians differ from one another, as do the members of any other body of people. They are not all highly intelligent, or extrovert, or wealthy. They are not all left-handed, or lorry drivers, or vegetarians. But there are many wonderful things that are true of every Christian in the world without exception, and we are going to look at four of these, all found in 1 Peter 2.9. Taken together, they vividly underline my first point, that there is no such person as an ordinary Christian. In fact, they mark out a Christian as a V.I.P. – a Very Important Person. Let us take them in order.

1. *THE CHRISTIAN'S DYNASTY* – 'But you are a chosen race. . . .'

When we hear a phrase like 'God's chosen race', or 'God's chosen people', our thoughts go straight to the people of Israel in the Old Testament: and of course that is where we find its origins.

When Abraham (Abram at the time, but we will use his later name for convenience) was seventy-five years old, God called him to leave home for a journey into the unknown. He had probably never heard of the land of Canaan that God promised to him; but his mind was filled with an even greater promise, God's word to him that 'I will make of you a great nation' (Genesis 12.2). Although childless, Abraham's obedience to the command, and his acceptance of the promise were immediate and total. The next chapters of Genesis unfold a story of such drama, adventure and courage as to make the most modern thriller read like a nursery rhyme by comparison. When he was a hundred years old, Abraham's wife Sarah gave birth to a son, Isaac, and at last the way seemed open for God's pledge to be fulfilled. Isaac would be the link between Abraham and the unborn generations to come who would form the 'great nation' God had promised. But Abraham's greatest test was yet to come. Unbelievably, God directed him to take Isaac and put him to death as a sacrifice on Mount Moriah. In a staggering act of obedience, Abraham took Isaac up the mountain, made an altar, bound Isaac upon it, and was about to plunge his knife into Isaac's body when God dramatically intervened. Abraham's faith had been proved, and the promise was immediately renewed: 'By myself I have sworn, says the Lord, because you have done this, and have not withheld your son, your only son, I will indeed bless you, and I will multiply your descendants as the stars of heaven and as the sand which is on the seashore. . . .' (Genesis 22.16–17).

The story then widens and develops in an amazing way. Isaac's twin son Jacob (whose name was later changed to Israel) had twelve sons, who eventually gave their names to the twelve tribes of the new nation. The new people's history now took an erratic and unstable course until they were swept off to captivity in Egypt for 400 years. Then came the remarkable story of the exodus under Moses, the forty years of wandering in the wilderness, and eventually the settlement in the promised land of Canaan.

That is the merest skeleton of the story – but through it all runs one central theme: God chose out a people for himself, and guided and guarded their ways until his purposes were fulfilled. Without this, the Old Testament is no more than a scrapbook of unconnected incidents; with it, the whole drama can be seen as one story, the story of God's dealings with his people.

Turning to the New Testament, we discover a phrase which links all of this with the point about Christians being 'a chosen race'. Paul says that although he is a full-blooded Jew, he has nothing in which he can boast spiritually 'except in the cross of our Lord Jesus Christ, by which the world has been crucified to me, and I to the world' (Galatians 6.14). He then goes on, 'For neither circumcision counts for anything, nor uncircumcision, but a new creation' (Galatians 6.15) – in other words, the rituals and ceremonies of the Old Testament are unable to make a person a Christian; he needs to be born again, to become 'a new creation'. Then comes the phrase we are looking for, for Paul immediately adds, 'Peace and mercy be upon all who walk by this rule, *upon the Israel of God*' (Galatians 6.16).

Here is the link between the drama of the Old Testament story and the life of a twentieth century Christian. Every Christian in the world today, whether Jew or Gentile by origin, is a member of the new, spiritual Israel – what Paul calls 'the Israel of God' – and as such part of the 'chosen race' of which Peter speaks. Have you ever grasped this before? If so, have you thought it through to an understanding of some of the implications that follow from it? Here are two of them.

Firstly, we are involved in the purposes of God.

In an itinerant ministry, I have the privilege of travelling to many famous places that I would not otherwise visit. To stand at Bannockburn, or on the Mayflower Steps in Plymouth, or under the shadow of the Berlin Wall, or at the Parthenon in Athens, or on the Golden Horn in Istanbul, or at the spot in Dallas where John F. Kennedy was assassinated, always fills me with a sense of history, a tingling knowledge that my own life is something more than an unconnected accident. But there is an even greater way in which we can experience a sense of history. Oliver Cromwell once said 'What is history but God's unfolding of himself?'; and someone else put it even more succinctly by saying that 'History is his-story'. History is the record of God at work; in the unknown reaches of the universe, in the world around us, in the whole vast human stage. John Stott has a superb comment on this point in his book *The Message of Galatians*. He writes: 'There is a great need in the church today for a biblical, Christian philosophy of history. Most of us are short-sighted and narrow-minded. We are so pre-occupied with current affairs in the twentieth century that neither the past nor the future has any great interest for us. We cannot see the wood for the trees. We need to step back and try to take in the whole counsel of God, his everlasting purpose to redeem a people for himself through Jesus Christ. Our philosophy of history must make room not only for the centuries after Christ, but for the centuries before him, not only for Abraham and Moses but for Adam, through whom sin and judgment entered the world, and for Christ, through whom salvation has come. If we include the beginning of history, we must include its consummation also, when Christ returns in power and great glory, to take his power and reign. The God revealed in the Bible is working to a plan. He "accomplishes all things according to the counsel of his will" (Ephesians 1.11).'

The Christian who knows his Bible can rejoice that in a very special way he is caught up in the purposes of God. His birth, life, conversion and circumstances are not accidents, nor the result of blind fate – they are part of history, and therefore part of 'his-story'. They are prepared, planned and purposeful. Bertrand Russell, the famous philosopher, once wrote 'You are an eddying speck of dust; a harassed, driven leaf' – but the Christian who knows his Bible knows better! He sees that he is part of God's eternal and unchanging purposes. As Matthew Henry put it, 'All true Christians are a chosen generation; they make one family, a sort of species of people distinct from the common world'.

This is the first thing that follows from the fact that Christians are described as 'a chosen race'. It means that if you are a Christian, you are linked to every other Christian in history, and are brought with them into the orbit of Paul's tremendous conviction that 'in all things God works for the good of those who love him, who have been called according to his purpose' (Romans 8.28 New International Version). What a secure philosophy of life to have in today's neurotic world!

Secondly, we inherit the promises of God.

While Mary was expecting the baby Jesus, she visited her near relation Elizabeth, who was later to become the mother of John the Baptist. In an extraordinary prophecy inspired by the Holy Spirit, Elizabeth told Mary that she was to be 'the mother of my Lord' (Luke 1.43). No doubt remembering an earlier promise made to her by an angel, Mary responded with the words we sometimes call 'The Magnificat', a great song of praise to God which ends 'He has helped his servant Israel, in remembrance of his mercy, as he spoke to our father, to Abraham and to his posterity for ever' (Luke 1.54–55). Notice that the promise made to Abraham was linked with the birth of Jesus and the salvation of believers. Immediately after the birth of John the Baptist, his father Zacharias, filled with the Holy Spirit, prophesied in words we sometimes call 'The Benedictus'. This is a pouring out of praise to God for the coming of Jesus into the world as Saviour, Redeemer and Lord, and it includes the very important words that in doing so, God was acting 'to perform the mercy promised to our fathers, and to remember his holy covenant, the oath which he swore to our father Abraham. . . .' (Luke 1.72–73). Again, the promise to Abraham, the coming of Jesus, and the salvation of his people, 'the Israel of God', are all linked together.

An Arab once told me of the importance of Abraham in Moslem traditions. There are apparently nearly 200 references to him in the Koran, the sacred book of Islam, and as a great prophet and leader he is referred to as the father of the faithful. But the Bible's teaching goes much further than that, and says that the true children of Abraham are those who share his faith, who trust in Abraham's God for salvation; *and that as such they inherit the promises of God*. Just as surely as the Christian has proved the promise of salvation to be true, so he can prove the truth of all the other promises that God makes to believers in his word. In C. H. Spurgeon's *The Chequebook of the Bank of Faith*, a book of daily Bible readings, he compares each of the Bible's promises to a cheque drawn in the Christian's favour and signed by God. All the Christian has to do is to take it, endorse it with his own name and 'come to heaven's bank in order to receive the promised amount'. That sounds too simple, but I am convinced that this question of active faith in the declared promises of God is a vital key to healthy, progressive Christian living. I once saw these words written on the wall of a church in Spokane, Washington: 'You can never starve a man who is feeding on the promises of God'. That is a change of metaphor from the one used by Spurgeon, but it is not a change of truth. If you are a Christian, you are a child of God, a member of his family, part of the 'chosen race', and as such, the promises of God are yours. Find them, know them, claim them and live in the proved experience of them! That is part of your heritage!

2. *THE CHRISTIAN'S DIGNITY* – '. . . a royal priesthood'.

Of the four phrases Peter uses in this verse, three are taken from Exodus 19.5–6, words spoken by God through Moses to the people of Israel at Mount Sinai. One of the titles given to them there was 'a kingdom of priests' (Exodus 19.6), and what makes this such a striking phrase is that throughout the Old Testament kings and priests held separate offices. In 2 Chronicles 26 there is a vivid illustration of the importance of this. King Uzziah was an outstanding leader who achieved unusual success as a military general and civil administrator. But later we read the fateful words 'But when he was strong he grew proud' (2 Chronicles 26.16). He began to throw his weight around, and to assume rights that were not his, even as king. One day, he went into the temple to burn incense on the altar, a function strictly reserved to the priesthood. Azariah, the high priest, rushed into the building with eighty fellow-priests and told Uzziah that he had usurped his authority, warning him to 'Go out of the sanctuary; for you have done wrong, and it will bring you no honour from the Lord God' (2 Chronicles 26.18). Caught in the very act of defying God's clear command, Uzziah was furious, but as the anger broke out in his heart, so, to the astonishment of everybody present, leprosy broke out on his forehead. He was immediately bundled out of the temple. His career was over, and he remained a leper until his dying day.

Nothing could demonstrate more vividly the clear distinction between the offices of king and priest under the Old Testament dispensation: yet here is Peter uniting both in describing a New Testament Christian. John does the same thing when he ascribes praise 'To him who loves us and has freed us from our sins by his blood and made us a *kingdom, priests* to his God and Father. . . .' (Revelation 1.5–6). Again, John tells us of those before the throne of God who sing praises to the one who has redeemed men to God 'and hast made them *a kingdom and priests* to our God. . . .' (Revelation 5.10). To go back to Peter's phrase, Christians form 'a royal priesthood'. Spiritually speaking, they have the dual dignity of being both kings and priests. What does that mean in practical terms?

Firstly, as a king you can exhibit God's power.

Of all the terms used in these studies, 'a king' surely seems the most difficult to accept and to demonstrate in practical terms. It sounds too good to be true. A bit of enthusiastic exaggeration, perhaps? A slight case of religious licence? Not a bit of it! Because a Christian is 'in Christ' (2 Corinthians 5.17) he shares all that Christ is. Christians will not only reign with Christ in the future – Paul says '. . . if we endure, we shall also reign with him. . . .' (2 Timothy 2.12) – they reign with Christ *now*. In his commentary on Revelation, Luther Poellot says that the kingdom to which Christians belong 'is Christ's kingdom of grace and glory. Its members have royal power and dignity. By faith they possess all that Christ, their one great King, has. They rule with him. They concur in all that he does. They do with him all that he does. They own the universe, the world, and all things in the world'.

Breathtaking stuff!

Let me try to be even more practical. A Christian reigns in a situation by overcoming it, by subduing it, by mastering it, by coming through it, by using it to demonstrate the grace and love and power and mercy of God. The Christian reigns by overcoming the world (1 John 5.4), by crucifying the flesh (Galatians 5.24) and by resisting the devil (James 4.7). The Christian is seen to reign as he demonstrates the all-sufficient power of God at work in his life.

Secondly, as a priest you can enter God's presence.

Under the old Covenant, no ordinary Jew was allowed to go beyond the Court of the Israelites in the temple. Only the high priest could go into the inner sanctuary, the Holy of Holies. In New Testament days, the way to the Holy of Holies in the temple in Jerusalem was barred by a huge curtain. At the moment of Jesus's death, there was a violent earthquake, and 'the curtain of the temple was torn in two, from top to bottom' (Matthew 27.51). It must have been a frightening moment for those in the temple at the time – but it symbolizes a glorious truth for every Christian in the world today. The writer to the Hebrews puts it like this: 'Therefore, brethren, since we have confidence to enter the sanctuary by the blood of Jesus, by the new and living way which he opened for us through the curtain, that is, through his flesh, and since we have a great priest over the house of God, let us draw near with a true heart in full assurance of faith. . . .' (Hebrews 10.19–22). Just as certainly as the curtain was torn away from the Holy of Holies on that historic day, so for the Christian the spiritual barrier that kept him from God has been torn away by the death of Christ. What is more, every Christian is ordained as a priest and is, as it were, officially authorised to come into the presence of God at any time, on any matter, in any circumstance.

When Access Credit Cards were launched in Britain, the great advertising slogan used was 'Access takes the waiting out of wanting'. The message was clear. Whatever you wanted, you could get immediately, by using your Access card. Without making an explicit comment on the philosophy that says 'Get whatever you want – now!', let me say that the Christian has an even better Access Card. Paul tells us about it when he says that in Christ 'we have boldness and *confidence of access* through our faith in him' (Ephesians 3.12). This 'card' may not always take the waiting out of wanting – in fact, it may at times take the wanting out of waiting! – but it does something much greater. It enables even the weakest Christian to bring all his needs, problems, fears, anxieties, sorrows and circumstances to God's throne of grace, knowing that there are sufficient resources there to meet his every need 'according to (God's) riches in glory in Christ Jesus' (Philippians 4.19). And those riches are not affected by a change of government, a credit squeeze, a pay pause, a mini-budget or a fall in share prices! As a priest, you have constant, immediate access to God by the prayer of faith. Let nothing rob you of this great privilege!

3. *THE CHRISTIAN'S DUTY* – 'a holy nation'.

The Amplified Bible translates this 'a dedicated nation', and perhaps this moves us a little closer to the two points I want to make here.

Firstly, it is a covenant duty.

The expression 'a holy nation' is another of the three

phrases taken from Exodus 19, where God's words were given in the context of the covenant he established with Israel. Under that covenant, God promised to pour out great blessings on his people, but as we know from the story that unfolds after that, Israel forfeited many of them because of their disobedience.

The lesson is clear. As we have already seen, God's promises remain – but so does the Christian's duty to obey God's revealed will. The Christian is under the moral obligations of God's law. He is free from the law as a system of salvation, but not as a yardstick of sanctification. *He is not forced to obey it in order to be saved; he is free to obey it because he is saved.* A new covenant assumes new conduct. As Paul puts it 'For God did not call us to be impure but to live a holy life' (1 Thessalonians 4.7, New International Version). Too many Christians seem to have missed their vocation. Not all Christians are called to be ministers, or evangelists, or similar public figures – but all Christians are called to live a holy life, a life that is morally superior to the rest of mankind.

This link between the Christian's covenant and call is seen again in the words immediately following the ones we are studying. Peter says that Christians are a chosen race, a royal priesthood, a holy nation and God's own people 'that you may declare the wonderful deeds of him who called you out of darkness into his marvellous light. Once you were no people but now you are God's people; once you had not received mercy but now you have received mercy' (1 Peter 2.9–10). As Alan Stibbs remarks in the Tyndale New Testament Commentary: 'So it is the company of erstwhile outsiders with no status and deserving judgment as sinners who, because of God's mercy towards them in Christ, and because they have come to him, are told that they now constitute a community characterised by election, royalty, priesthood, holiness and privileged relation to God as his special people. They are also told that what has thus happened to them, and what they now are by God's doings, is intended to proclaim or advertise to the universe the worthiness of God's works and ways'. That puts it precisely – and leads us on to notice that

Secondly, it is a constant duty.

Every year, the Movement for World Evangelization takes over Butlin's Holiday Camp at Filey, Yorkshire for a week's Christian Holiday Crusade. Within hours, a tremendous change comes over the camp. The dance halls become auditoriums for rallies, bars are transformed (perhaps converted would be a better word!) into offices and exhibition areas, the betting shop closes down, and so on. The Butlin's Camp staff have a phrase for this invasion. They call it 'Holy Joe Week'. There is no malice in the phrase, and perhaps it is an unconscious compliment. Things are different, to put it mildly! Bingo gives way to Bible study; punting to praying; and knees up at the dance to knees down in devotion! Yet no Christian should have a 'Holy Joe Week'. The Christian should never observe any week or day as especially 'holy' in moral terms, for the simple reason that his duty to live a godly life is constant. To call Sunday 'The Lord's Day' does not imply that the other six belong to someone else! Just as there is never a day when the Christian is not secure in his salvation, so there should never be a day when he should relax his sanctification. Christians are meant to constitute a nation characterised not by its formulae, rituals, or ceremonies, but by quality of life. As 'a holy nation' this is the Christian's duty.

4. *THE CHRISTIAN'S DESTINY* – '. . . God's own people. . . .'

A dictionary definition of 'destiny' is 'the purpose or end to which any person or thing is destined or appointed', and that is a good definition to hold in mind as we turn to this final phrase. The translations are interesting here. The Revised Version translates it 'A people for God's own possession', the Amplified Bible has 'God's own special purchased people', and the New International Version renders it 'a people belonging to God'. All these contribute something to our understanding of what Peter is saying. Let us draw from it all two strands of truth.

Firstly, there is a selection we cannot fathom.

In an earlier study, we came across Paul's statement that '. . . we were by nature children of wrath' (Ephesians 2.3). The point that he is making is brought out in a stunning way by the Amplified Bible's version: 'We were then by nature children of God's wrath and heirs of his indignation. . . .' Hold that terrible description – and remember that it is a description of everybody in the world – alongside the same version's rendering of our phrase here in 1 Peter 2.9, where Christians are called 'God's own special purchased people'. What a staggering thing! You were born 'a child of God's wrath and an heir of his indignation'; by the grace of God you have become one of his 'own special purchased people'! Can you understand that? Can you fathom it out? Johanna-Ruth Dobschiner was a fifteen-year-old Jewess when Hitler invaded Holland in 1940. By 1944 her parents and two brothers had been snatched away by the Nazis in their anti-Semitic purge. Johanna-Ruth went underground and, by one means or another, continued to escape the fate of thousands of her fellow Jews. She also came to know Christ as her Saviour. Her biography is called *Selected to Live* and, while the reference is primarily to her miraculous survival of the terrible processes of anti-Jewish activity in Europe during World War II, it is also a perfect description of what has happened to every child of God. A Christian has been selected to live; to live essentially in Christ, to live effectively for Christ, and to live eternally with Christ. Yet the Christian has yet to be born who can fathom out why this should be!

Secondly, there is a security which cannot fail.

In calling Christians 'God's own people', Peter is speaking not about a passing phase or experience, but a destiny; and for the Christian that means the certainty of spending eternity in heaven. The journey may be long or short, the road rough or smooth, our health good or bad, our work large or small – but our destiny is certain and assured. In Jesus's own words: 'In my Father's house are many rooms; if it were not so, would I have told you that I go to prepare a place for you? And when I go and prepare a place for you, I will come again and will take you to myself, that where I am you may be also' (John 14.2–3). God has not selected us merely to engage in his earthly programme, but to enjoy his eternal presence, and every Christian should seek to live in the conscious certainty that each day takes him nearer to that glorious experience. Can you remember when you last did that?

Several years ago I was at a youth rally which had as an item on its programme something called 'Desert Island Disciples'. The young people concerned had to answer questions about being shipwrecked miles from anywhere, and one was asked what his favourite hymn would be in that position. Quick as a flash he replied 'Lord, I'm coming home'! I thought that was a nice one! And by the grace of God it is a hymn that every Christian can sing every day, in spirit even if not in tune. If, like Abraham, we have responded to God's call, then like him, we are journeying into the unknown as far as this world is concerned. But like Abraham, we also look forward 'to the city which has foundations, whose builder and maker is God' (Hebrews 11.10).

It has been said that a man's life is influenced more by his expectations than by his experience. If that is so, what a vast difference there should be between the life of the Christian and that of the unbeliever! Here are two quotations, each from a person universally famous, and each speaking about his expectations:

'There is darkness without, and when I die there will be darkness within. There is no splendour, no vastness anywhere; only triviality for a moment, and then nothing.'

'For I am sure that neither death, nor life, nor angels, nor principalities, nor things present, nor things to come, nor powers, nor height, nor depth, nor anything else in all creation, will be able to separate us from the love of God in Christ Jesus our Lord' (Romans 8.38–39).

The first statement was made by Bertrand Russell. He was a peer of the realm, a philosopher, a scientist, a mathematician, a political theorist, and a Nobel Prize winner.

The second statement was made by the Apostle Paul – a real V.I.P.!

Chapter 8

A Christian

It came as a great surprise to me when I first discovered how seldom the Bible mentions the word 'Christian'. Today, we use it more than any other to describe a follower of Christ, and in addition we speak about 'the Christian Church', 'the Christian faith', 'the Christian way of life' and so on – yet the word 'Christian' occurs only three times in the whole Bible.

Surprise number two came after I had looked closely at these three references. Although the word 'Christian' was probably in common use both inside and outside the church by the middle of the first century, it is likely that in not one of the three places in which we find it in the Bible was it used by Christians themselves. The first reference is in Acts 11.26 where we read '.... and in Antioch the disciples were for the first time called Christians'. This almost certainly means that they were called Christians by other people, as a nickname or an easy means of identification. Then we come to Acts 26.28, where there is no doubt as to who used the phrase. It was the heathen King Agrippa who snorted at Paul 'In a short time you think to make me a Christian!' Finally, we have 1 Peter 4.16, where we read '. . . yet if one suffers as a Christian, let him not be ashamed, but under that name let him glorify God'. Peter has been speaking about the oppression and reproach Christians would have to suffer 'for the name of Christ' (1 Peter 4.14). They were being linked with a Galilean trouble-maker called Jesus who claimed to be 'the Christ', yet who could not even offer a defence at his trial on a charge of blasphemy and was eventually executed by Pontius Pilate with the overwhelming consent of the man in the street. To get tied up with a man like that was to risk all kinds of trouble.

That, then, seems to be the way in which the word came into use, and this suggestion is confirmed by the fact that about the year 116 AD the Roman historian Tacitus wrote about the persecution by the Emperor Nero of those 'who the populous, or common people, were calling Christians'. The word 'Christian' was clearly a nickname, a term of abuse, associating people with an allegedly deluded Galilean preacher. Then something wonderful happened. The followers of Jesus took this derogatory nickname and began to use it among themselves. Soon, it became a standard word of identification. They took the mud slung at them by their enemies and fashioned it into a badge of honour, to be worn with pride. Today, there is no better name that can be found for those who trust Christ as their Saviour, acknowledge Christ as their Lord, and serve Christ as their King. A Christian is a Christian! – and as we take a closer look at the places where the word is used in the New Testament three important truths will emerge, helping us to consolidate the answer to our question 'What in the world is a Christian?'

1. *A MAN UNDER INSTRUCTION.*

'. . . and in Antioch the disciples were for the first time called Christians' (Acts 11.26). It seems to me that the crucial point here is clear and obvious on the surface of the text. Those called Christians by unbelievers were known as disciples by the believers. The words 'Christians' and 'disciples' are synonymous. Mark that! I remember as a young Christian sometimes being harangued from the pulpit along these lines: 'You may be a Christian, but are you a disciple? You have begun the Christian life, but have you gone on to that higher stage?' That sounded very challenging, and therefore healthy, stimulating and beneficial. But I have since come to the conclusion that it is nothing of the sort. We need to beware of enthusiasm that is not controlled by the guidelines of Scripture. Zeal alone is not necessarily a good thing. It broke Paul's heart to realize that many Jews had 'a zeal for God, but it is not enlightened' (Romans 10.2). The thought of an express train roaring along at 100 m.p.h. sounds like exciting fun – but not if it has left the rails! In the same way, challenging people to a higher plane of Christian living sounds marvellous – but not if the way being taught has no basis in Scripture.

The Bible knows nothing of a rigid, two-tier system of Christianity, whether the leap on to the upper platform is alleged to be brought about by a special experience of some kind, or by particular knowledge, or by an emphasis on some point of doctrine. Likewise, the Bible nowhere makes a distinction between a disciple and a Christian. What we do find – as our verse here in Acts 11 makes crystal clear – is that the two words describe the same people. All the disciples were Christians; all the Christians were disciples. So one way of asking 'What is a Christian?' is to ask 'What is a disciple?'

The answer to the question put that way is perfectly straightforward, because the word 'disciple' simply means 'a learner'. The disciple is a pupil, a man under instruction. When people speak about 'the disciples' they usually mean either the twelve men specially selected by Jesus, or the seventy who were sent out by him, or those who were gathered together on the day of Pentecost. But the Bible mentions the word in a much wider context than that. We read of the 'disciples of Moses' (John 9.28), and of 'the disciples of John (the Baptist)' (Matthew 9.14). We are told that '. . . the Pharisees . . . sent their disciples to him. . . .' (Matthew 22.15–16). In both the Greek and Jewish worlds, philosophers and teachers gathered to themselves groups of trainees, who sought to understand their line of teaching. They were men under instruction, and the common word for them was 'disciples', so the word was a natural one to use about the people who attached themselves to Jesus, and sought to follow his teachings. Now let us develop the idea a little further, because when we examine what the Bible has to say about the disciples of Jesus, we find two particular characteristics demanded of them.

Firstly, a determined acquisition of the truth.

On a visit to Macedonia, I was taken to visit a Christian

102

recovering in hospital from a serious operation. As we approached the ward, I was told that this man was an elder in the church in Berea. Immediately, my mind flew to the verse where we are told that the Jews at Berea 'were more noble than those in Thessalonica, for they received the word with all eagerness, examining the Scriptures daily to see if these things were so' (Acts 17.11). I had hardly finished locating the quotation in my mind when we rounded the corner and stepped into the ward – and there was the man from Berea propped up in bed, reading his Bible! The New Testament had come to life! Here was a worthy successor of those noble Bereans. He had a hunger for God's Word, like David who cried 'How sweet are thy words to my taste, sweeter than honey to my mouth!' (Psalm 119.103). The mark of a genuine disciple is that he is determined to acquire the truth – and not merely thoughts about the truth. We are living at a time when that will bear repeating. Although we are being deluged with one new Bible translation or paraphrase after another, I am not convinced that today's rising generation of Christians know their Bibles any better. There is a difference between being able to express general ideas of what we might call Christian philosophy, and knowing what God's Word says. I remember having impressed upon me as a young Christian the value of memorising Bible passages, but that seems to be going out of fashion today – and many people are losing out as a result. David was able to say 'I have laid up thy word in my heart, that I might not sin against thee' (Psalm 119.11). Can you say that? Are you laying up God's Word in your heart? Are you taking time to learn and to know your Bible? Are you determined to acquire its truth? Or are you settling for vague religious slogans?

Not that a knowledge of Scripture comes easily. Salvation is by faith, but knowledge of the Bible is by works! Jim Elliot, who was martyred by the Auca Indians in Ecuador in 1956, once said this: 'I find I must drive myself to study, following the "ought" of conscience to gain anything at all from the Scripture, lacking any desire at times. It is import-ant to learn respect and obedience to the "inner must" if godliness is to be a state of soul with me. I may no longer rely on pleasant impulses to bring me before the Lord. I must rather respond to principles I know to be right, whether I feel them to be enjoyable or not'. *I would suggest that you read that paragraph again*, because it contains a vital key to spiritual progress. The disciple must learn to obey what Jim Elliot called the 'inner must' in order to acquire the truth of the Word of God.

Secondly, a diligent application of the truth.

This takes the issue a vital stage further, and the crucial verse on the subject is where Jesus says to the Jews who had believed on him, 'If you continue in my word, you are truly my disciples. . . .' (John 8.31). The Amplified Bible fills out the meaning like this: 'If you abide in my word – hold fast to my teachings and live in accordance with them – you are truly my disciples'. It is not open to a disciple to pick and choose what he hears, or the teachings with which he will agree, or by which he will live. A disciple is not like a scholar facing an examination and needing to attempt only five questions out of ten. Biblically, he is expected to acquire all that he can, and to apply everything that he acquires.

Jesus pressed this point home in a number of ways. In John 10, for instance, he said: 'My sheep hear my voice, and I know them, and they follow me'. There is the dual response of hearing and following. As Al Martin has put it, 'The sheep had an open ear and an obedient foot' – and what is true of the sheep should be true of the scholar, the disciple. Then Jesus spoke of Christians being like branches of a vine, adding, 'By this my Father is glorified, that you bear much fruit, *and so prove to be my disciples*' (John 15.8). Again, the picture is clear. The branch is expected to bear the same fruit as the parent tree, and the Christian is expected to live out what he draws in. Then again, speaking to his disciples in the upper room at Jerusalem, Jesus said 'A new commandment I give to you, that you love one another; even as I have loved you, that you also love one another. By this *all men will know that you are my disciples*, if you have love for one another' (John 13.34–35). The same point comes through loud and clear. Only by a diligent

104

application of the truth does a man prove his Christian discipleship. Knowing the truth is not enough; there must be doing as well.

Following Britain's entry into the European Common Market, a British civil servant was discussing with a friend the difficulties of having to learn a new language. 'Oh, I'm all right,' his colleague replied. 'My French is excellent,' adding rather apologetically, 'except for the verbs!' Well, you can imagine how he would get on without verbs! Grammatically speaking, a sentence is incomplete without a verb; and spiritually speaking a man's profession to be a Christian is invalid unless it has verbs to back it up. The genuine disciple, the true Christian, is recognised not merely as someone who acquires truth, but who applies it diligently in his life, proving his faith by his actions. As James puts it: '. . . be doers of the word, and not hearers only, deceiving yourselves' (James 1.22). A Christian, then, is a disciple, a man under instruction.

2. *A MAN UNDER IMPULSION.*

'And Agrippa said to Paul, "In a short time you think to make me a Christian!" ' (Acts 26.28).

The confrontation between Agrippa and Paul was rather like the one between David and Goliath. Herod Agrippa the Second was the great grandson of Herod the Great, and a special favourite of the Emperor Nero, and had even changed the name of Caesarea Philippi to Neronias in the Emperor's honour. At the time of the incident at which we are going to look, he was on a State visit with his queen Bernice (who was also his sister) to Porcius Festus, Procurator of Judea. Festus was holding the Apostle Paul on three charges – treason, being the ringleader of an unauthorised rebel organisation called the Nazarenes, and defiling the temple. The case had dragged on for about two years, and had now reached a crucial point, because Paul had suddenly upset the apple-cart by exercising his right as a Roman citizen and demanding to be tried in Rome before the Emperor Nero himself. This presented Festus with a tricky problem, because while he would want to frame a report that would infer his wide knowledge about the case, he was in fact woefully ignorant about the ramifications of Jewish religious law. Suddenly, there was a ray of light! Agrippa was an expert in Jewish religious affairs. For twenty years he had had the prerogative of appointing the Jewish High Priest in Jerusalem. What is more, he had expressed a wish to see and hear Paul for himself. Festus suddenly realised that by arranging a meeting between Agrippa and Paul, he could neatly kill two birds with one stone.

With great pomp and ceremony, Agrippa and Bernice took their places in the audience hall, alongside Festus, the Army's top brass and all the civic superstars. The whole glittering assembly settled into their places. Enter Paul!

Although we have no further details of the scene, it is not difficult to picture Paul weary and gaunt after two years in prison. Many deduce from certain parts of his Epistles that he suffered from failing eyesight. Similarly, it is thought that he was not particularly handsome in general appearance; some people find evidence that he had an unimpressive voice and a rather poor manner of delivery. But as soon as Agrippa says 'You have permission to speak for yourself' (Acts 28.2) the whole balance of power changes dramatically.

Paul is suddenly clothed with authority and holy boldness. With devastating clarity he presents his case, marshalling his facts like a brilliant lawyer. Even a bad-tempered interruption by Festus fails to divert him, and at the end of the day even Agrippa has to admit to Festus, 'This man could have been set free if he had not appealed to Caesar' (v. 32). It is a fascinating incident – but it is also much more than that. It is not only a narrative that lets us hear Paul's words, it is an X-ray that enables us to see into his heart, and what we see is an overriding concern not merely to prove the merits of his case but to proclaim the message of his Saviour.

He begins by saying 'I am to make my defence today. . . .' (v. 2) but for Paul the best method of defence was attack, a positive declaration of the Gospel. Eventually he looks straight at Agrippa and challenges him: 'King Agrippa, do you believe the prophets? I know that you believe' (v. 27).

This provokes Agrippa's testy reply: 'In a short time you think to make me a Christian!' Paul's answer to that tells us everything: 'Whether short or long, I would to God that not only you but also all who hear me this day might become such as I am - except for these chains' (v. 29). Here was a man under impulsion - the impulsion of the gospel. Paul was no pussyfooting apologist. He did not content himself with superficial consent to a vague theological concept. He had met with Christ, and from then on he was a man under impulsion. When writing of this to the church at Corinth, he said 'For Christ's love compels us . . .' (2 Corinthians 5.14, New International Version), or, as the Amplified Bible puts it, '. . . controls and urges and impels us'. The New English Bible puts it even more directly: '. . . leaves us no choice'. Christ's amazing love in dying for sinners on the cross was the inextinguishable fuel that fed the flames of Paul's magnificent obsession. It was this which demanded his soul, his life, his all. As Alan Redpath puts it in his book *Blessings out of Buffetings*: 'Paul had looked with Spirit-enlightened eyes into the heart of God, and Christ's love for him gripped him, propelled him, impelled him along one line of life to the exclusion of any other attraction'. Let me underline this in two ways.

Firstly, he had an impulsion to give out.

It is a well-known criticism of many Christians today that they are like the Canadian rivers in winter - frozen at the mouth! Exactly the opposite was true of Paul and the other apostles. When the news of the resurrection of Jesus shook Jerusalem, the local authorities became very agitated about the apostles' preaching, and ordered them 'not to speak or teach at all in the name of Jesus' (Acts 4.18). The reply Peter and John gave could not have been clearer: 'Whether it is right in the sight of God to listen to you rather than to God, you must judge; for we cannot but speak of what we have seen and heard' (Acts 4.20). Inevitably, they were soon in trouble again, on the same charge. 'We strictly charged you not to teach in this name, yet here you have filled Jerusalem with your teaching . . .' the high priest thundered. The apostles reply was firm and final: 'We must obey God rather than men' (Acts 5.29). That, for them, was the crucial issue. There was no way around it. They were under divine orders to preach, and no human authority could change that. No wonder we read that at the end of the session '. . . they left the presence of the council, rejoicing that they were counted worthy to suffer dishonour for the name. And every day in the temple and at home they did not cease teaching and preaching Jesus as the Christ' (Acts 5.41–42). That same impulsion gripped Paul. His own testimony could not be clearer: 'For if I preach the gospel, that gives me no ground for boasting. For necessity is laid upon me. Woe to me if I do not preach the gospel!' (1 Corinthians 9.16).

So, faced with the combined pomp and power of Festus and Agrippa, Paul cannot hold back. He has to speak the truth, not out of human enthusiasm for a religious cause, but as what a friend of mine used to call 'the natural outcome of a spiritual income'. To go back to an earlier metaphor, Paul did not have the impediment of an icy mouth, but the impulsion of a heart on fire. He was swept along by what Thomas Chalmers called 'the expulsive power of a new affection'. He had to tell of the one who had conquered him by love. Do you share anything of that divine impulsion? Is sharing the gospel with others a drudge, a duty – or a delight? Are you motivated by a church programme, or by an overwhelming sense of the love of Christ in dying for you and for others on the cross of Calvary? To answer those questions is to take your own spiritual temperature!

Secondly, he had an impulsion to get through.

Leighton Ford has written a book on the priority of evangelism under the title *The Christian Persuader*. That is a fine title, because it comes straight from the pages of the Bible. In that same passage from which we quoted earlier, Paul says that the nub of the Christian's ministry was this: 'we persuade men' (2 Corinthians 5.11). What he is saying is that this is our business, our commission, our concern, our aim. For Paul, it was not sufficient to get things said; he was not satisfied until they were heard, understood and obeyed. There is a perfect example of this when he tells the Christians at Rome that '. . . we have received grace and apostleship *to bring about the obedience of faith* for the sake of his name among all the nations . . .' (Romans 1.5). Paul's attitude was not 'There is the message. Take it or leave it'. *He had to get through*, and he was willing to do anything in the will of God that would help to imprint the relevance of his message on the hearts of his hearers. He even dares to say this to unconverted Jews: 'Christ knows and the Holy Spirit knows that it is no mere pretence when I say that I would be willing to be damned for ever if that would save you' (Romans 9.3, The Living Bible).

It is almost impossible to grasp the brilliance of what Paul is saying here, which makes a complete mockery of Agrippa's outburst, accusing Paul of thinking that he could make him a Christian as the result of just a few minutes' work. As Paul quickly showed him, time or effort were immaterial. He would gladly have spent all that he had of both if it meant the conversion of one more sinner. He was driven by an impulsion to get through.

In a book called *The Company of the Committed*, Elton Trueblood has suggested that most of the evangelistic similes Jesus used had this theme of penetration. He goes on: 'The purpose of salt is to penetrate the meat and thus preserve it. The function of light is to penetrate the darkness. The only use of keys is to penetrate the lock. Bread is worthless until it penetrates the body. Water penetrates the hard crust of the earth. Leaven penetrates the dough to make it rise.' Does this say anything about your evangelistic concern? In New Testament terms, a Christian is a man under impulsion, a man who has a message to give, and who is determined to take it to a world in need.

3. *A MAN UNDER INVASION*.

'. . . yet if one suffers as a Christian, let him not be ashamed, but under that name let him glorify God' (1 Peter 4.16).

To say that a Christian is a man under invasion immediately after saying that he is a man under impulsion may sound like a contradiction. But it is not. A Christian invades and is invaded; he attacks and is attacked. He is commanded to go into the world, and at the same time to prevent the world from getting into him. No New Testament writer is clearer or more insistent than Peter on the point that a Christian is under invasion in this world. He warns Christians that they 'may have to suffer various trials' (1 Peter 1.6). He tells of situations where Christians will 'do right and suffer for it' (1 Peter 2.20). He warns them that they may 'suffer for righteousness' sake' (1 Peter 3.14) and be 'reproached for the name of Christ' (1 Peter 4.14). He tells his readers that 'Your adversary the devil prowls around like a roaring lion, seeking someone to devour' (1 Peter 5.8). He prophesies the danger of 'false teachers among you, who will bring in destructive heresies' (2 Peter 2.1) and 'exploit you with false words' (2 Peter 2.3). He tells Christians to be prepared to face ridicule by 'scoffers . . . following their own passions' (2 Peter 3.3). He tells them to 'beware lest you be carried away with the error of lawless men and lose your own stability' (2 Peter 3.17). One has only to read those phrases to see that this was one of Peter's major themes and concerns – and perhaps that is hardly surprising. After all, he would vividly remember Jesus saying to him, 'Simon, Simon, Satan demanded to have you, that he might sift you like wheat' (Luke 22.31). He would remember how he had boasted to Jesus, 'Though they all fall away because of you, I will never fall away' (Matthew 26.33), only to be swept to the ground by the devil's cunning a few hours later. He would remember other attacks, too, by both religious and civic authorities. Peter knew what the inside of a prison cell looked like. He knew the biting pain of being lashed by the triple-thonged scourge, under which Paul had nearly died. Yes, Peter was qualified to write as he did about the Christian being a man under invasion. But what are the lessons for us? Here are two.

Firstly, expect invasions as being usual.

Earlier in the chapter Peter writes 'Beloved, do not be surprised at the fiery ordeal which comes upon you to prove you, as though something strange were happening to you' (1 Peter 4.12). A Christian may be surprised by the timing or direction of a spiritual attack upon him, but he should never be surprised by the *fact* that he is attacked. The devil may change his tactics, but never his principles. He thrives on attack! Paul tells us that every temptation that comes to the Christian is 'common to man' (1 Corinthians 10.13). Those three words are just one in the Greek – *anthropinos*, which literally means 'of man', or 'human'. In other words a Christian must expect these things. There is nothing strange about them. They are inevitable. They are part of the human scene. I wonder if you have noticed a little phrase in Acts 14 that bears this out exactly. Paul and Barnabas had been teaching new converts in Lystra, Iconium and Antioch, and in the course of what they said they encouraged them 'to continue in the faith . . .' (Acts 14.22). That is exactly what we would anticipate them saying in that situation – but the verse does not end there! It goes on – '. . . and saying that through many tribulations we must enter the kingdom of God'. Not 'we *may*', but 'we *must*'. There is no such thing as an easy Christianity. *If it is easy, it is not Christianity; if it is Christianity, it is not easy.* Living as we do in the alien environment of a godless world, there is no way in which we can escape being attacked. To recognise this is to build a barrier against depression and despair when the going gets tough. Especially if you are a young Christian, settle it in your mind here and now that the going *will* be tough. And the closer you seek to follow Christ, the closer you will get to the centre of the devil's target area!

Secondly, accept them as being usable.

In *As You Like It*, Shakespeare makes the Duke say:
>'Sweet are the uses of adversity
>Which, like the toad, ugly and venomous,
>Wears yet a precious jewel in his head'.

That is not the only place where Shakespeare captured a profound truth about life, but if we turn to the Bible instead of the bard we have this particular point on much better authority. In the Sermon on the Mount, Jesus says 'Blessed are you when men shall revile you and persecute you and utter all kinds of evil against you falsely on my account. Rejoice and be glad, for your reward is great in heaven, for

111

so men persecuted the prophets who were before you'
(Matthew 5.11–12). Here is one picture of the Christian
under invasion, under attack. He is being persecuted and
reviled. Every kind of evil is being said against him because
of his stand as a Christian. What Jesus tells us is that when
that kind of thing happens to us, we are to use it as a means
of helping us to contemplate and rejoice in the eternal glory
and reward that will be ours in heaven, and as a means of
confirming in our hearts that we are following in the foot-
steps of the great men of God who also suffered for Christ's
sake. Only the Christian is able to do that! When the unbeliever gets hit, and gets hurt, his only responses are to hit
back, to 'grin and bear it', or to grow bitter and depressed.
But the Christian can actually take the most savage attack
and use it as a theme for an anthem of praise to God.

The Apostle James gives us a similar picture: 'Count it all
joy, my brethren, when you meet various trials, for you
know that the testing of your faith produces steadfastness.
And let steadfastness have its full effect, that you may be
perfect and complete, lacking in nothing' (James 1.2–4).
Here again, notice that trials are usable. They test a man's
character. They help him to grow spiritual muscle. They
develop and deepen the fibre of his personality. Without
pressure, a Christian would grow feeble and flabby. Only as
he faces up to life's problems, and learns to overcome them
will he grow to spiritual maturity. Happy the Christian who
sees every trial as a means to that great end!

Paul, too, says much the same sort of thing. When God
showed him that his thorn in the flesh was not going to be
removed, he said 'I will all the more gladly boast of my
weaknesses, that the power of Christ may rest upon me. For
the sake of Christ, then, I am content with weaknesses,
insults, hardships, persecutions, and calamities; for when I
am weak, then I am strong' (2 Corinthians 12.9–10). What
Paul is saying is that these pressures and trials enabled him
to recognise just how frail and helpless he was, *and that they
did something else*. They forced him to stop trusting in his
own power, ability, eloquence, enthusiasm or courage, and
to trust instead in the all-sufficient grace of God made

112

available to him in Christ. Here is a fascinating and frightening insight into the human heart. Given half a chance, we jump at every opportunity of proving that we can 'go it alone'. We are incurably proud of our own ability to cope. And often it is only when we find our defences cracking, and our resources dwindling that we turn to the Lord and call upon him. When attacks do that, they do us a great service! They become usable. They open a gateway to the grace of God.

So in this passage, Peter says, 'But rejoice in so far as you share Christ's sufferings, that you may also rejoice and be glad when his glory is revealed. If you are reproached for the name of Christ, you are blessed, because the spirit of glory and of God rests upon you' (vv. 13–14). As with Jesus, James and Paul, Peter sees the Christian's suffering as being usable. He sees it as a means of reminding the Christian that just as he is sharing Christ's sufferings now, so he will share Christ's glory in the world to come. What is more, to suffer as a Christian is to know the assurance of the Holy Spirit's presence in one's heart, and the outworking of his power in one's life. If only Shakespeare had known!

Expect attacks as being usual; accept them as being usable. That, in a nutshell, should be the Christian's philosophy as he faces the trials, temptations and pressures of living in today's evil world. Moreover, he should do so in the unshaken conviction that even the worst attack, the most violent persecution, the most sickening body-blow, the most subtle trial, only comes to him under the sovereign hand of God, and can therefore be turned to his praise. As John Hercus puts it in *Pages from God's Casebook*: 'The great blows of God are designed to stand a man up, to awaken him from the dream-world of his tiny humanity, and make him take his place as an "image of God", as a creature made in the likeness of God'. In other words, they are designed to make a Christian *be* a Christian!

Chapter 9

'. . . as he is . . .'

It was to be John 17 tonight – yet again! Our informal
evening discussions on this chapter had only been meant to
last for a few nights, but somehow those of us sharing that
lovely house party at the little Spanish resort of Palamos
could not get away from it. Early in that night's session,
somebody remarked on the number of times the words
'glorify' or 'glorified' appeared in the chapter, and we began
to pick them out. Verse 1, for instance, then verse 4, and
verse 5. Next, we came to verse 10, and I began to read aloud
these words spoken by Jesus to his Father in heaven –
'all mine are thine, and thine are mine, and *I am glorified in
them*'. Immediately, a hush came over the room. Nobody
spoke, nobody moved. It seemed for a few moments as if
nobody breathed, either. Those five words had stunned us
into silence. The effect they had was literally breathtaking. I
can sense it again even as I write. Here was Jesus saying that
he was glorified in the lives of Christians, that in some
mysterious, majestic way, honour was brought to his name
by ordinary, everyday believers. I forget how the discussion
went from then on, but it was a long time before we got away
from that staggering revelation.

There are other verses in the Bible that have had the same
kind of effect on me over the years. Ephesians 1.18, for
instance, where Paul, speaking of the Lord Jesus Christ,
refers to 'the riches of his glorious inheritance in the saints'.
Earlier in the same chapter he speaks of the Holy Spirit as
'the guarantee of our inheritance' (v. 14) – and we can perhaps begin to understand what that means. But to speak of
us as Christ's 'glorious inheritance' is surely bewildering in
its impact.

Then there is John's marvellous prophecy that when Jesus returns to the earth 'we shall be like him, for we shall see him as he is' (1 John 3.2). A missionary was once translating the first Epistle of John with the help of a native teacher. When they came to these words, the native laid down his pen and said 'No, I cannot write these words. It is too much. Let us write "We shall kiss his feet" '. Yet in the wonder of God's love it is *not* too much. It is the certain fulfilment of Christ's redeeming work for every believer – 'we shall be like him'.

But it is another verse from that same epistle that is going to occupy our attention in this study, and this is how it reads: 'In this is love perfected with us, that we may have confidence for the day of judgment, because *as he is so are we in this world*' (1 John 4.17).

As I went through my Bible seeking answers to the question 'What in the world is a Christian?' I felt that it was impossible to escape this verse. Frankly, I would have done so if I could – not because I did not believe it, but because I could not understand how such a thing could be true. I wrestled and prayed with these nine words for hours, and more than once I very nearly laid them aside altogether. But finally I was drawn back to them, and I believe that there are truths here that I can share with you as a means of blessing and encouragement.

We are going to look at the whole verse in this study, but let us begin by concentrating on those critical last nine words: 'as he is, so are we in this world'. What is your immediate reaction to a statement like that? Mine is to protest 'It's not true. I am *not* like Jesus in this world. It is the constant concern of my heart that I am so utterly *unlike* him'. And surely that kind of reaction is backed up by Scripture? Towards the end of even his remarkable life, Paul admits 'Not that I . . . am already perfect; but I press on to make it my own . . .' (Philippians 3.12). Again, writing to the Christians at Corinth, he speaks of the process of sanctification like this: 'And we all, with unveiled face, beholding the glory of the Lord, are being changed into his likeness from one degree of glory to another; for this comes from the Lord who is the Spirit' (2 Corinthians 3.18). Paul says that we 'are *being changed*' into Christ's likeness, not that the process is complete and that we can claim to be Christ's moral equals. Even for the very best of Christians, sanctification is an uncompleted process.

Knowing these things as I did, it was hardly surprising to find this verse perhaps the most tantalisingly difficult I had ever sought to study. Yet as I prayed over it and weighed it up I came to the conclusion that it summarises the whole five chapters of this epistle, in the sense that it consists of the three themes that occupy most of John's attention as he is writing. Beyond any doubt, those themes are *love, assurance* and *fellowship*. To put it statistically, these three words are mentioned about sixty times in 105 verses, or more than once in every other verse of the epistle. Bearing that in mind, glance again at 1 John 4.17. *Love* is obviously the subject in the opening phrase: 'In this is love perfected with us'; *assurance* is the point of the second phrase: 'that we may have confidence for the day of judgment'; and, as we shall see in a moment, *fellowship* is at the heart of the final phrase: 'as he is so are we in this world'.

Now let us turn to our study of the text itself. If we begin with the final phrase (which is the key to the whole verse), we discover that John is speaking of

1. *OUR COVENANT POSITION* – '. . . as he is, so are we in this world.'

We can only begin to unravel the meaning of these words when we understand that John is not suggesting that any Christian is of the same moral quality as Jesus. Even the grammar begins to point us to that conclusion, because it speaks of 'as he *is*', and not 'as he *was*'. John is not making a point of comparison between the kind of life that Jesus lived when he was on earth, and the kind of life we as Christians are living now. Anybody who compares himself with Jesus in those terms does so as the result of ignorance or insanity. The Beatles made a big thing some time ago about their being more *popular* than Jesus, but the point was completely irrelevant. Even if they were, what would it prove? Jesus never set out to be popular, or to supply what people wanted. Before he ever came into the world he knew that he would be 'despised and rejected by men' (Isaiah 53.3), and just before he left it he told his followers that the world at large 'have seen and hated both me and my Father' (John 15.24).

John is not, then, suggesting that we are morally as good as Jesus – but he *is* saying something even more wonderful – that *God treats us as if we were!* To appreciate how this can possibly be so we need to get to grips with one of the greatest themes in the Bible, the doctrine of imputation. 'To impute' is a legal phrase. It means to reckon, or to take into account. It is to assume and declare a person to be in a certain position as far as you are concerned, and then to deal with them on that basis. A. A. Hodge says that to impute means 'to lay to one's charge as a just ground for legal procedure'. That may sound terribly dull, but it prepares the ground for us to understand one of the most fundamental and exciting lines of truth in the whole Bible, which tells us that three things that are imputed in the spiritual world. We are mainly concerned with the third, but will glance at the other two in passing.

Firstly, Adam's sin was imputed to mankind.

This is how Paul puts it: '. . . sin came into the world through one man and death through sin, and so death spread to all men because all men sinned. . . .' (Romans 5.12). When Adam first sinned he brought the whole human race into a state of sin and under the judgment of God, *because he was the human race*, and the federal head of all of his successors. As Paul adds, '. . . by one man's disobedience many were made sinners. . . .' (Romans 5.19). Even more concisely, he tells the Corinthians that 'in Adam all die' (1 Corinthians 15.22). There, in four words, you have positive proof of the truth of imputation. The fact that all men die is proof that they are in Adam, that they share in the result of his fall into sin.

Secondly, the sins of believers were imputed to Christ.

This is where theology becomes exciting! Speaking on

117

behalf of all Christians, Peter is able to say 'He (Christ) himself bore our sins in his body on the tree' (1 Peter 2.24). The phrase he uses here does not mean that Christ bore or carried our sins away (although that is wonderfully true) but rather that he actually bore or carried them *upon himself*. As Paul puts it, 'God made him who had no sin to be sin for us, so that in him we might become the righteousness of God' (2 Corinthians 5.21, New International Version). To use a different picture, our sins were charged to Christ's account. He accepted responsibility for them in terms of the judgment due for them. He agreed to pay the penalty that we had incurred. To quote Paul again, 'Christ redeemed us from the curse of the law, having become a curse for us – for it is written, "Cursed be everyone who hangs on a tree" ' (Galatians 3.13). We can never fully understand the wonder of this, but let us at least try to grasp the fringes of its meaning. A Christian's sin is removed and forgiven not because God set aside his justice in favour of his love, nor that God makes exceptions to his law that all sin must be punished with death. In the death of Jesus the Christian's sin *was* punished, the full penalty of God's law was paid, and his justice totally satisfied. Our sin was imputed to him. As someone once put it:

> Because the sinless Saviour died,
> My guilty soul is counted free;
> For God, the Just, is satisfied
> To look on him, and pardon me!

Thirdly, the righteousness of Christ is imputed to believers. This is the other side of the wonderful picture of our salvation. Not only is our guilt transferred to Christ, but his obedience and merit is imputed to us. Paul not only says that '. . . by one man's disobedience many were made sinners', but he adds that 'by one man's obedience many will be made righteous' (Romans 5.19). That 'one man' is, of course, the Lord Jesus Christ, and what Paul is saying is that Christ's righteousness is credited to the Christian. He brings the same amazing truth into his own testimony when he speaks of himself as 'not having a righteousness of my own, based on

118

law, but that which is through faith in Christ, the righteousness from God that depends on faith' (Philippians 3.9).

That, in a nutshell, is the imputation of Christ's righteousness to the Christian. Notice very carefully that just as our forgiveness does not mean that God has denied that we were ever guilty, so our being counted by God as righteous, and being dealt with by him on that basis, does not mean that God says we are righteous *in ourselves*. There is no ground for boasting here. As Louis Berkhof puts it: '. . . the divine declaration is not to the effect that these sinners are righteous in themselves, but that they are clothed with the perfect righteousness of Jesus Christ. This righteousness wrought by Christ is freely imputed to them . . . and all to the glory of God'.

Now I have called this situation of our guilt transferred to Christ and of his righteousness transferred to us *our covenant position*. Let me explain this as briefly as possible. The Bible teaches that even before the world was made, God the Father and God the Son entered into a covenant of grace to bring about the salvation of all believers. There are many references to this in the Old Testament. In Psalm 2, for instance, we have, as it were, a snatch of conversation in which God the Father speaks to the Lord Jesus and says 'You are my son, today I have begotten you. Ask of me, and I will make the nations your heritage, and the ends of the earth your possession' (Psalm 2.7–8). We can link that kind of prophecy with verses like Ephesians 1.4 where Paul tells us that God 'chose us in him (Christ) before the foundation of the world'. Here is the heart of the whole miraculous drama of man's salvation, and no words can adequately put it into one brief statement. But let me attempt it like this: Before the world began, God determined to redeem a people unto himself, to put away their sin, and to restore the broken relationship it caused. This was expressed as a covenant, something that God decreed would be done. In this covenant, Christ acts as the Representative of all those to be saved. In their place he meets all the moral demands of God's law and atones for their sins by bearing the punishment that was due to them. No wonder the writer to the

119

Hebrews says that 'This makes Jesus the surety of a better covenant' (Hebrews 7.22)!

To see even that flimsy outline of God's wonderful plan of salvation is to get further than many Christians ever do in understanding their position in Christ. Is it beginning to fit into place in your mind and heart? Because you are in Christ, the moral demands of God's law can no longer harass you, and the penal demands of God's law can no longer threaten you! You should hardly be able to keep your seat for excitement at reading that! No wonder David cries out 'Blessed is he whose transgression is forgiven, whose sin is covered. Blessed is the man to whom the Lord imputes no iniquity, and in whose spirit there is no deceit' (Psalm 32.1–2)!

After that piece of theological deep-sea diving, let us come up for air and see what it teaches us about the meaning of John's phrase 'as he is, so are we in this world'. If I had to reduce it to one word, I would use the word '*accepted*'. On the basis of the covenant, decreed by God the Father, carried out by God the Son, and applied to our hearts and lives by God the Holy Spirit, we have become 'accepted in the Beloved' (Ephesians 1.6, AV). It is impossible to put the Christian's security more clearly or firmly than that. As surely as Christ's saving work was accepted by God the Father as meeting the demands of the law and the terms of the covenant, so we are accepted, because we are 'in Christ'. To give an expanded paraphrase of the words we are studying, 'As he is (accepted by God the Father) so are we (accepted by God the Father) even though we are still living in this world'. Surely this is the real heart of what John means when he writes 'our fellowship is with the Father and with his Son Jesus Christ' (1 John 1.3). This is our covenant position. We can now go on to link this with another part of the verse we are studying. This tells us of

2. *OUR CONFIDENT PRIVILEGE* – '. . . that we may have confidence for the day of judgment'.

We have already seen that as Christians our covenant position is that we are 'in Christ'. We are accepted in the Beloved, we have *fellowship* with the Father and with his Son Jesus Christ. We are now going to see that our privilege is to have a happy *assurance* that we are saved and secure in Christ.

In the church's history, one of the great debating points in the realm of personal salvation has been the question of the relationship between salvation and assurance. Many ecclesiastical worthies have got very hot under their dog collars arguing whether assurance was *part* of salvation (that is to say of the essence of it) or whether it was something quite separate from it, though closely linked. In other words, is it possible to have one (salvation) without the other (assurance)? Is it possible to be saved and not be sure that you are saved? Must a person know that he is saved before his salvation can be real? Or, looking at it the other way round, can we say that a person who has no assurance is not in fact saved?

You may never have given a great deal of thought to the matter – and if not, beware of giving an immediate answer to the questions! Even great giants of the church have given vent to strange statements on the subject. John Calvin, for instance, contradicted himself more than once on the subject of salvation and assurance; and Martin Luther is on record as saying 'he who hath not assurance spews faith out'! Methinks he has since changed his mind!

What is clear is that there is a great need for sound teaching on the subject. A lack of understanding about biblical assurance of salvation has become the father of a horde of ill-behaved children in the Christian church today. Too many Christians seem convinced about their doubts, and doubtful about their convictions. The story is told of the building of a lighthouse on a bleak headland on the coast of America. After a great deal of work, the great day came for the opening of this brilliant new aid to navigation, and with the day came the thickest fog seen in those parts for years. Two old Red Indians stood nearby as the opening ceremony was held, and when it was all over one turned to the other and said, 'Waste of money. Horns blow, bells ring, lights

121

flash, but fog come in just the same!' We have never had so many horns blowing, bells ringing and lights flashing as we have in the church today, and perhaps we have never had so much fog either! Yet whereas so many Christians are confused on the subject, the Bible is so clear. John speaks about having 'confidence for the day of judgment'. He is so sure of what he is saying that he speaks of assurance not merely in terms of the here and now, but in terms of that day when 'God judges the secrets of men by Jesus Christ' (Romans 2.16).

But to answer that historical teaser! Is assurance *essential* to salvation? No! No! A thousand times no! Let me give you three reasons why this must be the case, and allow you to fill in the remaining 997!

Firstly, because the object of our faith is Christ, not any emotions or actions on our part, and the two are quite distinct. Imagine that you are on a train journey from London to Glasgow. After an hour or two you feel tired, and decide to have a nap. A few minutes later you have lost all consciousness that you are on board a train – but it does not affect the fact that you are! You may be asleep, but you are not lying on the sleepers! Your body is still committed to the train, regardless of your feelings or emotions on the issue. In the same way, it is the *fact* of trusting Christ that brings a man salvation, not his *feelings* about it.

Secondly, the Bible teaches that Christians are to be 'all the more eager to make your calling and election sure' (2 Peter 1.10) – the obvious inference being that it is possible to behave in such a way, or to neglect the means of grace so seriously, that a Christian becomes unsure of his calling and election. Notice carefully that it does not say that a man's calling and election can be forfeited – that is absurd and impossible – but that a man can lose the sense that they are *sure*.

Thirdly, there is the honest testimony of those of God's people, throughout the Old Testament, on into the New Testament, and right down the long years of the church's history, who have found themselves wrestling with doubt and insecurity. Some of the greatest Christians have been shaken

122

with doubts and fears about their salvation at some stage of their lives – but nobody assessing their lives seriously questions the reality of their salvation.

But having said all that, we must add this: *a happy assurance of salvation is both possible and desirable*. It is the ideal. It is the biblical norm. It is what God intends. Paul's prayer for the Christians at Rome was this: 'May the God of hope fill you with all joy and peace in believing, so that by the power of the Holy Spirit you may abound in hope' (Romans 15.13). John goes so far as to say that this is one of his main purposes in writing this first epistle: 'I write this to you who believe in the name of the Son of God, that you may know that you have eternal life' (1 John 5.13).

This, then, is the confident privilege that God wants us to enjoy; a settled, balanced, calm assurance that we are right with God, not on the basis of anything that we are in ourselves, or of anything that we have achieved, but because we are 'in Christ'. If you have any personal doubts about this, then get before the Lord in prayer. Ask him to help you to understand the facts about your salvation, and to grant you that work of the Holy Spirit in your heart which Paul describes as 'the Spirit himself bearing witness with our spirit that we are children of God' (Romans 8.16).

And one word of warning: there is a world of difference between assurance and presumption. It is idle for man to boast 'I am saved' unless he can prove it by his life. I remember a man who runs boys' camps during the summer holidays recalling how one of the lads had once said to him 'What you tell us confirms what we see'. That was a significant statement! The boy had put one and one together! The teaching corresponded with the lives of the camp leaders. This is the biblical pattern. Creed and conduct should look alike. As James puts it, 'For as the body apart from the spirit is dead, so faith apart from works is dead' (James 2.26). A genuine Christian has both, and to rejoice in his salvation is his confident privilege.

So far, we have looked at what our verse has to say about two of John's major themes – *fellowship* and *assurance*. Now we can pick out the third, *love*, as we consider

3. *OUR CONSTANT PRIORITY* – 'In this is love perfected with us.'

Let us begin by noticing that John speaks of love as a developing moral quality of life. He says 'In this is love *perfected* . . .', and the word means 'brought to completion'. In the previous verse, he speaks of God's love *to* Christians: 'So we know and believe the love God has for us . . .'; now he speaks of God's love at work *through* Christians, reflected and developed in our lives. There is a vitally important link here. Throughout this epistle, the Christian's assurance is linked with the moral qualities of his life, and the quality most often singled out is *love*. John says 'We *know* that we have passed out of death into life, because we *love* the brethren' (1 John 3.14). Further on, he adds 'Little children, let us not *love* in word or speech but in deed and in truth. By this we shall *know* that we are of the truth . . .' (1 John 3.18–19). Sometimes, he puts the point the other way round, and says that the man without love is the man without God. For instance, he says quite bluntly 'He who does not love does not know God; for God is love' (1 John 4.8), and illustrates this later when he writes 'If any one says "I love God" and hates his brother, he is a liar; for he who does not love his brother, whom he has seen, cannot love God whom he has not seen' (1 John 4.20).

John has hammered home his point both positively and negatively. Love is the distinguishing mark of the Christian. It is a kind of test. He says in effect that not only can a man without love have no Spirit-given assurance of his relationship with God, but that that relationship does not exist. If we can put a wide-angle lens on this for a moment, we will see something else, and that is that people who are not Christians will judge us at this very point. Jesus makes this quite clear when he says 'By this all men will know that you are my disciples, if you have love for one another' (John 13.35).

It is this verse that is taken up so effectively by Dr. Francis Schaeffer in his book *The Church at the End of the Twentieth*

Century. He has a chapter called 'The Mark of the Christian', in which he says: 'Jesus gives the world a piece of litmus paper, a reasonable thermometer. There is a mark which, if it cannot be seen by the world, allows them to conclude "This man is not a Christian" '. He does go on to admit that the world may be mistaken in its judgment, because although we are Christians we are still human, we make mistakes, we are capable of failing, we love imperfectly. But this in no way lessens the impact of what he is saying. Jesus has given the world the right to make a judgment about our Christian profession *on the basis of our love*. Our theological grasp, our organising ability, our qualities of leadership, our eloquence, our loyalty to the church – all of these things are irrelevant in the world's eyes. The size of your church, the number of big evangelical names you can drop, the number of committees on which you sit, your acceptability as a speaker, the popularity of your music – you can forget about those things at this point. They are purely secondary when it comes to the world making a judgment about your spiritual standing, and to the question of your influence in drawing men to Christ. What the world sees, and knows, and recognises and needs is *love* – and it is on that basis that it makes its response.

Surely that makes love our constant priority? When Mother Teresa of Calcutta was in London receiving an award for her humanitarian work in India, she said 'The biggest disease is not leprosy, or tuberculosis, but rather the feeling of being unwanted, uncared for, deserted by everybody.' People suffering from that disease are to be found not only on the streets of Calcutta, but in the offices, factories, shops, board rooms, schools, universities and homes of our own country, and the only person capable of showing truly biblical love towards them is the Christian in living touch with the Lord. We must seek in every way we can to be the kind of people who can make a valid claim that 'God has poured out his love into our hearts by the Holy Spirit, whom he has given us' (Romans 5.5, New International Version). To fail here is to fail completely in our witness to the world, and to risk producing the kind of response captured in these very pointed words which I once found pinned to a school notice-board under the title 'Listen, Christian':

> I was hungry,
> And you formed a humanities club
> And discussed my hunger.
> Thank you.
>
> I was imprisoned,
> And you crept off quietly
> To the chapel in your cellar
> And prayed for my release.
>
> I was naked,
> And in your mind
> You debated the morality of my appearance.
>
> I was sick,
> And you knelt and thanked God for your health.
>
> I was homeless,
> And you preached to me
> Of the spiritual shelter of the love of God.
>
> I was lonely,
> And you left me alone to pray for me.
>
> You seem so holy,
> So close to God,
> But I'm still very hungry,
> And lonely,
> And cold.
>
> So where have your prayers gone?
> What have they done?
> What does it profit a man
> To page through his book of prayers
> When the rest of the world
> Is crying for his help?

You may feel that some of those words are a little cynical – but there is greater pain in recognising that they may reflect the truth! The Christian is not only called to *be* good, but to *do* good, and to fail in the latter is automatically to fail in the former.

And there is a price to be paid. When the Marechale, daughter of General Booth the founder of the Salvation Army, was asked the secret of her power, she replied 'First, love; second, love; and third, love. And if you ask me how to get it, I answer "First, sacrifice; second, sacrifice; and third, sacrifice" '. That takes us straight to the words of Jesus when he said 'Greater love has no man than this, that a man lay down his life for his friends' (John 15.13). When Jesus spoke these words, he was obviously referring to his own impending death on the cross. Today, it is almost always used in the context of war, or the defence of law and order. But the words have another significance, and the previous verse tells us what it is.

Jesus said 'This is my commandment, that you love one another as I have loved you', and when we link this with his next words we see that for us today true love involves the sacrifice of self on behalf of others. It means being willing to deny yourself, your own pleasures, your own ambitions, anything that centres on yourself, for the blessing and well-being and benefit of others – even those who are your enemies. In his book *The Royal Route to Heaven*, Alan Redpath comments on this verse in the context of the Christian's influence on the unconverted, and what he says is deeply challenging: 'That is the principle upon which you are called to live as a child of God in the light of the cross; to lay down your life for your friends, to forfeit things you may consider to be perfectly legitimate in order that your friends may find the way to Jesus more easily.' That, ultimately, is the supreme sacrifice. Without wanting to be in any way insensitive, I believe that the sacrifice of *self* is more costly, and even more difficult, than the sacrifice of one's body. The sacrifice of dying physically is, of course, unspeakable, and one that we cannot possibly understand. But there is a sense in which we are called upon as Christians to make an even greater sacrifice while we live; we are called upon to sacrifice ourselves for the blessing of others.

Only as we are prepared to make that sacrifice will we rightly reflect the one who 'though he was rich, yet for your sakes he became poor, so that by his poverty you might become rich' (2 Corinthians 8.9). We will never be able to match his love, but we are called upon to mirror it, and to do so as a constant priority.

What in the world is a Christian? Someone in the covenant position of being accepted in Christ; someone who can have an assurance of this as a confident privilege; someone who is called upon as a constant priority to reflect the love of Christ by sacrificing self for the blessing of others.

Chapter 10

'... many other words...'

There is a story about a man in America found guilty of a serious offence and sentenced to ninety-nine years' imprisonment. In any circumstances the sentence was severe, but this particular man had an additional problem – he was eighty-seven at the time! When the sentence was announced, he looked despairingly at the judge and cried 'But your Honour, I will never be able to complete it all!' 'Never mind', the judge replied kindly, 'just go away and do as much as you can'!

To condense the Bible's answer to the question 'What in the World is a Christian?' into less than 200 pages presents a similar problem, and all that we have been able to do in these studies is to uncover some of the facts. Yet perhaps it has given us a starting-point for further work, deeper study, and greater rewards as we explore God's Word in our own individual ways.

Acts 2 records what happened on the Day of Pentecost, and includes a summary of Peter's sermon on that day. I have called it a summary, because it is obvious that not every word he spoke is recorded. Indeed we are specifically told that '. . . he testified with *many other words* . . .' (Acts 2.40). In the same way the Bible has 'many other words' to answer our question. Some of them are scattered widely throughout the New Testament. Christians are described as 'ambassadors' (2 Corinthians 5.20); 'believers' (1 Timothy 4.12); 'branches' (John 15.5) and 'aliens and exiles' (1 Peter 2.11). At other times several words are found close together. For example, you will find a Christian described in six different ways in the first two verses of Paul's Epistle to Philemon.

In this study, we are going to look at six different descriptions of a Christian clustered together in 2 Timothy 2. But let me first remind you of a principle that has run right through these studies, and that is that all doctrine is meant to lead to moral action. Let me put it like this: all the Bible's words for a Christian are nouns, obviously; but they should all lead to verbs, *naturally*! Each one of them suggests things we should be, or not be, do or not do. Hold this carefully in mind as we go through Timothy's 'Polyphoto' album of a New Testament Christian. In each case, we are going to make just one point of application, and, as it happens, it will always be in the negative. But to continue the photographic metaphor, there is nothing wrong with that, because the only way to get a good positive is to begin with a good negative. Eight of the Ten Commandments in Exodus 20 are in the negative, but what a contribution they make to positive Christian living! 'You shall not kill' safeguards a man's life; 'You shall not commit adultery' safeguards his marriage; 'You shall not steal' safeguards his property; 'You shall not bear false witness' safeguards his reputation, and so on. A good, strong negative prepares the way for a good, strong positive. Bear that in mind as we turn now to this great chapter, and note these six definitions of a Christian.

1. *A CHRISTIAN IS A SOLDIER – HE MUST NOT GET DIVERTED.*

'No soldier on service gets entangled in civilian pursuits,

since his aim is to satisfy the one who has enlisted him' (2 Timothy 2.4).

We have already devoted a chapter to the Christian as a soldier, but this verse gives me an opportunity to underline one point that is not difficult to apply today. Too many of our churches are like battalions of 'Dad's Army' – full-time civilians, but only part-time soldiers, with their time and interest solely taken up with furthering their own ends and following their own inclinations and interests, rather than seeking to have a single eye to God's glory. The story is told of a watchmaker who enrolled in one of the armies fighting in the American Civil War. At one stage, the war got bogged down, and there was a long lull in the fighting. Soon, a table in his tent was filled with watches, springs, wheels and all the other bits and pieces you would expect to find on a watch-maker's bench. His fellow-soldiers brought their watches to him for repair, and soon he was engrossed in his trade. But suddenly, the war sprang to life again, and his regiment was given the order to move. Everybody sprang into action except the watchmaker. Noticing this, another soldier burst into his tent and shouted 'Get up from there. Haven't you heard the orders. We're moving!' 'I can't', the man replied, 'I've got all these watches to repair.' He had for-gotten the real objective of his being there, which was not to repair watches, but to be a vital part of the fighting machine, ready and alert to obey every order of his commanding officer. In the same way, many Christians seem to have for-gotten why they have been called up. There is more to being a Christian than attending services and rallies, reading and praying, singing in a folk group, handing out tracts, or writ-ing out cheques for missionary societies. All of life is meant to be part of a Christian's active service – business and leisure, at work and at home, in public or in private. All of life is to be seen as a responsibility to please the one who has called us to be soldiers. Every part of life should be marked O.H.M.S. – On His Majesty's Service.

It is so easy to get our eyes off life's real purpose and on to secondary issues. Like everyone else, a Christian is involved with business matters, material and financial issues, family life, leisure time, social and community involvement, and many other legitimate issues. But Paul's point is that they are not pre-eminent. In ultimate terms they are secondary, in that they are to be conducted under the umbrella of the one great principle – that the Christian must please the Commanding Officer of his life. Paul went so far as to say that his great concern was simply that 'Christ will be honoured in my body, *whether by life or by death*' (Philippians 1.20). Notice that last phrase! As far as Paul was concerned, things like business success, popularity, wealth, health or even life itself were secondary matters. They were expendable. The only thing that mattered was that he brought glory to Christ, that he pleased him. As Vance Havner comments, 'We do not have to live; we have only to be faithful'.

Seneca, the famous Roman philosopher and adviser to Nero once said 'To live is to be a soldier'. For the Christian, to live is to be a soldier of Christ; which means that whatever happens, he must not get diverted from life's one great aim, which is that the Lord's name should be glorified in all that he is and does.

2. A CHRISTIAN IS AN ATHLETE – HE MUST NOT BREAK THE RULES.

'An athlete is not crowned unless he competes according to the rules' (2 Timothy 2.5).

This is not Paul's only use of a sporting metaphor. In an earlier letter he tells Timothy that 'bodily training is of some value' (1 Timothy 4.7), and in 1 Corinthians 9.24–27 he speaks about boxing and running. He uses the same two sports elsewhere when he says 'I have fought the good fight, I have finished the race' (2 Timothy 4.7).

The writer of the Epistle to the Hebrews uses very similar language when he says '. . . let us run with perseverance the race that is set before us' (Hebrews 12.1), and if we put this alongside the other references by Paul we find all the obvious lessons to be drawn – determination, discipline, dedication, and so on. But notice carefully that none of these is the point

131

that Paul is making here. What he does say is that no athlete is crowned 'unless he competes according to the rules'. What does he mean?

The picture itself is perfectly obvious. The athlete who cuts across the corner of the track, or pushes another competitor over would obviously be disqualified. In some sports the rules seem cruelly strict. The great American golfer Tom Weiskopf was disqualified from the 1974 World Open Golf Championship for the technical offence of failing to sign his card at the end of a round. If a man is to succeed, the rules must be kept. But what about the spiritual application?

This would not seem to be quite as obvious and straightforward, although we can begin by clearing away two negative points. In the first place, nobody becomes a Christian by keeping the rules, that is to say, by keeping God's law. The Bible clearly teaches that 'a man is not justified by works of the law' (Galatians 2.16). Nor does anyone remain a Christian by keeping God's law, or by leading an especially good moral life. A Christian is both saved and kept by the grace and power of God, and in no way by his own effort or achievement. We can be quite clear on those two points before we go any further.

The key to understanding what Paul is saying here is to see it in the context of Christian service. Elsewhere he speaks of receiving 'the crown of righteousness, which the Lord, the righteous Judge, will award me on that day, and not only to me, but also to all who have loved His appearing' (2 Timothy 4.8). James says that after a man has been tested he will receive 'the crown of life, which God has promised to those who love him' (James 1.12). In the same way, Peter tells the elders among the people to whom he writes that 'when the Chief Shepherd is manifested you will obtain the unfading crown of glory' (1 Peter 5.4). While all Christians will be crowned with the full experience of eternal life in heaven, some Christians will be particularly honoured as the result of their life, experience and service. That seems to be Paul's emphasis here. Notice. however, an important difference between the metaphor and the application. On the race-track only one athlete can gain the winner's prize (the laurel wreath as it would have been in Paul's day). But in the Christian race the crown will go to many, *provided they keep to the rules*. But what are they?

We are not told in this chapter, but in my view the answer lies along these lines. In Mark 12 the scribes asked Jesus which was the first (or the greatest) commandment of all. In reply Jesus said: 'The first is, "Hear, O Israel: The Lord our God, the Lord is one; and you shall love the Lord your God with all your heart, and with all your soul, and with all your mind, and with all your strength'. The second is this, "You shall love your neighbour as yourself". There is no other commandment greater than these' (Mark 12.29–31). In condensing the whole moral law of God into these two phrases, Jesus is saying that *the Christian's rules are the rules of love*. The Christian is blessed and rewarded not when he performs his religious rituals as a formal mechanical routine, but when his worship is a genuine experience of his love, what someone has called a time-exposure of his soul to God. The Christian service that God has pledged himself to honour and reward is not that done as a clinical duty, or motivated by a vague humanitarianism, but that done with love as its supreme motive.

For the Christian, the law of life is to be the law of love. That may sound trite – but it is far from easy. Unless we are very careful, we can find ourselves doing the right things for the wrong reasons. Look honestly at your Christian service. Why are you doing it? Is it in any measure to promote yourself, or your church, or your favourite youth organisation, or missionary society? Can you truthfully say that your Christian service is motivated by a deep sense of love for the Lord, and for the people you are seeking to serve in his name?

3. A CHRISTIAN IS A FARMER – HE MUST NOT EVADE THE BURDEN.

'It is the hard-working farmer who ought to have the first share of the crops' (2 Timothy 2.6).

Responsibility and reward are the two things that stand

out clearly here, and we can look at them in that order.

Firstly, there is responsibility.

Notice that Paul specifies 'the *hard-working* farmer'. Some years ago, I remember a preacher startling his congregation by suddenly announcing, 'I think I ought to warn you that I am about to use a four-letter word. It may offend some people. Indeed, some people don't ever want to hear it said in their presence. They don't want anything to do with it. But I'm afraid that I must use it, and here it is. . . .' The atmosphere was electric! Everybody tried to shrink back into their seats and look either disinterested or aghast. 'The word', the preacher went on, 'is *work*'. The gasps of relief could be heard a mile away!

But the preacher had a point! For too many Christians today, work is as unsavoury as a swear-word, with the result that the average church is suffering from a terrible imbalance among its membership – too many shirkers and not enough workers.

I am always reminded of this when making a plane journey. When there are, say, 100 people on board the aircraft, they are divided into something like ninety passengers and ten crew members. Now there is nothing wrong with the proportion of crew to passengers in that situation, but when we find the same thing in a church, then something *is* wrong. Switching quickly to Paul's illustration – which is much more down-to-earth! – he sees the ideal Christian as being like a hard-working farmer. Having spent many days and nights on farms all around the country, I have come to the conclusion that Paul would have been hard-pressed to find a better picture. William Barclay has said 'The farmer knows no hours', and from what I have seen, the demands on a farmer's time are as severe as on a doctor's. There is no hour of morning, noon or night when the farmer might not be called upon to do some urgent work – and he must never evade the burden.

The task facing the church today is overwhelming, but as ever 'the labourers are few' (Matthew 9.3). When a little boy was asked what his favourite part of the Bible was, he replied 'The bit where everybody loafs and fishes' – and I am afraid

134

that there are too many pew-polishers who share his view today. What is *your* personal commitment to the task of evangelism, to the ministry of your church, to the spiritual needs of your neighbours? Are you a labourer or a loafer? As long ago as 1906, Dr. G. Campbell Morgan was able to say at the Keswick Convention: 'Any man or woman in the church who does not know what it is to share the travail that makes his kingdom come, is dishonest and disloyal to Jesus Christ'. Those words bear repetition today! Whole-hearted commitment to the work of God's kingdom is our inescapable responsibility as Christians.

Secondly, there is reward.

Paul says that the hard-working farmer 'ought to have the first share of the crops'. The immediate meaning seems to be that Paul was telling Timothy that he was entitled to an adequate financial reward from the people he was serving. Paul's convictions about this were so firm that he was able to write to the church at Corinth: 'the Lord commanded that those who proclaim the gospel should get their living by the gospel' (1 Corinthians 9.14). Although he waived his rights and worked with his own hands to avoid certain local problems, he writes to Timothy clearly and on divine authority. Point in passing: how can churches, missionary societies and evangelistic agencies pay their workers an adequate salary in an inflationary situation unless Christians increase their giving to keep pace with it?

Yet there is a wider, spiritual application to this. Paul says that the hard-working farmer should get the first share of the crops, and the Bible teaches that in God's economy *he does*. The man who works hard and loyally at the impulse of the Holy Spirit is given rewards far beyond those that can be put into his wallet or deposited with a Building Society. This follows from the unshakable biblical law that *God honours obedience*: 'he who looks into the perfect law of liberty, and perseveres, being no hearer that forgets but a doer that acts, he shall be blessed in his doing' (James 1.25). God says plainly '... those who honour me I will honour ...' (1 Samuel 2.30). There is a spiritual law that operates in the realm of Christian service, by which God has sworn to

135

honour and bless the man who submits to him and serves him in selfless obedience. Referring to our verse about the farmer, William Hendriksen comments, 'Similarly, if Timothy (or any worker in God's vineyard) exerts himself to the full in the performance of his God-given spiritual task, he, too, will be the first to be rewarded. Not only will his own faith be strengthened, his hope quickened, his love deepened, and the flame of his gift enlivened, so that he will be blessed "in his doing" (James 1.25), but in addition he will see in the lives of others (Romans 1.13; Philippians 1.22, 24) the beginnings of those glorious fruits that are mentioned in Galatians 5.22–23.'

But only the Christian who is willing to share the burden will share the blessing. A barren life is often the result of idle hands. A Christian is a farmer, and he should not evade the burden.

4. *A CHRISTIAN IS A WORKMAN – HE MUST NOT BE CARELESS.*

'Do your best to present yourself to God as one approved, a workman who has no need to be ashamed, rightly handling the word of truth' (2 Timothy 2.15).

The point about hard work, and the reward that comes from it, has been made in the previous section. Here, in likening a Christian to a workman, Paul goes on to deal with two quite different issues.

Firstly, the workman's aim.

The workman is to present himself to God 'as one approved' and he must have 'no need to be ashamed'. It may be that the first phrase refers to his standing before God and the second to his standing before his fellow men. In any event. the particular work that Paul is about to mention is to be done in such a way that it meets with the approval of both God and man. There is a lovely parallel of phrases in Romans 14.17–18, where Paul says that 'the kingdom of God does not mean food and drink, but righteousness and peace and joy in the Holy Spirit; he who thus serves Christ is *acceptable to God and approved of men*'. That should be

136

the aim of every Christian in his daily living and service.

But we must add a rider to that principle. Where the two conflict, then the Christian's course is equally clear: 'we must obey God rather than men' (Acts 5.29). When a situation arises in which we cannot at one and the same time meet with both God's approval and man's, we are to forfeit the latter in order to ensure the former.

Yet whenever we can, we are to do our utmost to win God's approval and man's acceptance. To be rejected or criticised by our fellow men does not automatically mean that we must be acting in the right way! This, of course, is the line taken by the heretical Jehovah's Witnesses: often, when I have stood with them on my doorstep and strongly rejected their teaching – and particularly their blasphemous denial of the deity of Christ – they have told me that they are in no way surprised at my attitude, and that it helps to confirm their belief that they are true servants of God, because he promised that his servants would be rejected! That kind of reasoning is nonsense, of course. My neighbour would be angry with me if I started hurling bricks through the windows of his house, but his anger would hardly prove that I was acting biblically!

Our aim in all that we do is firstly to have God's approval, and then to act in such a way that when our motives and methods and manner are honestly examined by our fellow men, we have no need to be ashamed.

Secondly, the workman's actions.

Paul mentions one in particular here: 'rightly handling the word of truth'. The Authorised Version has 'rightly dividing the word of truth', and in some senses it is a better word. The root of the word means 'to cut', or 'to cut through' or 'to cut across'. It is the kind of word that would be used about ploughing a furrow in the field, or squaring off a particular piece of stone so that it would fit precisely into a building. In both cases, great care is needed to ensure that the thing is done accurately.

Now it is this kind of word that Paul uses in writing to Timothy, who had responsibility for teaching a group of local believers the word of God. If you glance at verses 17–18, you

137

will see that Paul refers to Hymenaeus and Philetus who had *'swerved from the truth* by holding that the resurrection (of the body) is past already'. Paul's great concern was that, in his ministry, Timothy should plough a straight furrow of biblical truth.

As a seven year old boy, I was evacuated from Guernsey just before the German soldiers landed at the beginning of World War II, and eventually found myself living on a farm on the Isle of Islay, in the Inner Hebrides. I was to be there for five years, during which time I found myself doing almost every kind of farm work. On one occasion the farmer humoured me by letting me try my hand at ploughing. He manoeuvred the horse and plough into position at the edge of the field, planted me between the plough handles, and stood back. My big moment had come! Eyes sparkling with anticipation, I clicked the reins, signalling the horse to start. The beast responded with a sickening lurch that almost tore my arms from their sockets! I clung to that plough as if it were my last stitch of clothing, but from the moment it moved it was completely out of my control. At a speed that would have won it the Derby by several lengths, the horse charged across the field, dragging one plough and one terrified boy in its erratic wake, while the farmer stood convulsed with helpless laughter. There could also have been just the suspicion of a smile on the horse's face!

That incident is a vivid illustration to me of what Paul is saying in this verse. Just as a plough needs to be handled by someone physically equipped to make sure that it makes a straight furrow, so God's Word must be interpreted and taught in a way that is honest and accurate. This would have a particular relevance for Timothy, of course, in his position as a leader, but it is not difficult to apply its lesson more widely. The Bible is not a general basis for discussion, or a collection of ideas open to private interpretation and adaptation. It is the living Word of God, and if a person aspires to teach its meaning to others, he should remember that he will need both inspiration and perspiration! It is not enough to throw off some general religious philosophy mixed in with a few random texts. Every Christian who seeks to teach the

138

truth of God's Word to others should do his utmost to understand its meaning precisely, and to preach its truth unashamedly, with the twin aims of the glory of God and the blessing of men. The person who thinks that he can get away with less might be well advised to read Jeremiah 48.10!

5. A CHRISTIAN IS A VESSEL – HE MUST NOT GET POLLUTED.

'In a great house there are not only vessels of gold and silver but also of wood and earthenware, and some for noble use, some for ignoble. If any one purifies himself from what is ignoble, then he will be a vessel for noble use, consecrated and useful to the master of the house, ready for any good work. So shun youthful passions and aim at righteousness, faith, love, and peace, along with those who call upon the Lord from a pure heart' (2 Timothy 2.20–22).

In the verses immediately before these, Paul pictures the church as 'God's firm foundation' or, as we might put it, a firmly founded building or house. In the verses now before us, Paul moves his camera indoors and says that in a large house you would expect to find a great variety of utensils, some made of gold or silver, and others of meaner material, depending on their purpose. The parallel today would be a collection of items ranging from a silver tea service to a plastic waste paper basket. And, Paul infers, the same is true in the visible church. It contains a bewildering variety of people, as we know only too well. Some are holy saints; others are hardened sinners. Some are a joy to the heart; others are a pain in the neck.

But having given us that picture, Paul forgets about the vessels and concentrates on the people they represent. As Donald Guthrie puts it in the Tyndale New Testament Commentary, 'The illustration in fact digresses in its application. The variety of vessels in the house is intended to show the variety of types in the church, but the application fastens on the people and the vessels are completely forgotten'. Yet Paul does aim in one clear direction: he calls for vessels that are purified, consecrated and useful to the master of the house. Just as the Christian soldier is to aim at pleasing the one who has called him, and the Christian workman is to seek the Lord's constant approval, so the Christian vessel must avoid pollution in order to be ready for the Master's use. Of the many things that are capable of polluting a Christian's life, and therefore affecting his usefulness in the Lord's service, two arise from this passage.

Firstly, wrong doctrine.

Nothing is taught more firmly or frequently in this Epistle than the value of sound doctrine and the dangers of false doctrine, and there seems to be an indirect reference to the same subject here. The Amplified Bible, translating part of verse 21, speaks of the man who 'separates himself from contact with contaminating and corrupting influences', and we can tie that in with what Paul said a little earlier about Hymenaeus and Philetus, who had swerved from the truth, were spreading false doctrine, and undermined the faith of some of the believers. The Christian has a constant responsibility not only to avoid false teaching, but to avoid compromising association with false teachers.

Of course this is easier said than done. In my own ministry I find that I have to walk a constant tightrope between being involved in the total work of the church, and not compromising with those who do not hold to the basic truths of the gospel. 'Speaking the truth in love' (Ephesians 4.15) is not as easy as just speaking the truth, or speaking in love! I must leave you to work out the implications of this in your own situation, and I ought to warn you that the application may be painful and difficult. Yet only by keeping unpolluted by false doctrine and compromising association with false teachers will the Christian be 'ready for any good work'.

Secondly, wrong desires.

Paul puts this quite bluntly: 'shun youthful passions'. William Hendriksen suggests that these are pleasure, power and possessions: pleasure in the sense of an inordinate craving for the satisfaction of bodily appetites such as food and sex; power in the sense of the drive to be superior, to lord it over everybody else; and possessions in the sense of a pre-occupation with material things. Be that as it may, we should bear in mind that Timothy was about forty years of age when this Epistle was written, and Paul's concern was obviously that he should be on his guard against the things most likely to grip him at that age in his life and at that stage of his ministry.

The lesson is obvious: *know yourself*. Recognise your weaknesses, your danger spots, the things that let you down, the weak spots in your own personality, and keep close to the Lord for his particular help at those points.

I wonder if I am an unusual preacher in not having my study walls festooned with texts? I have all sorts of other bits and pieces, of course, and one of these is a plaque of Achilles, a legendary Greek figure from Homer's Iliad. When he was a baby, and thought likely to die, his mother dipped him in the waters of the River Styx, since it was believed that no weapon could harm a body that had been covered by its waters. But in dipping the baby in the water, his mother held him by the heel, and the waters did not flow over that one part of his body. In later life, during a fierce battle outside the gates of Troy, an arrow from the bow of the god Apollo struck him in that one unprotected spot, and Achilles died of the wound. Only a legend? Yes, but a legend with a lesson. I can never look at that plaque on my study wall without being reminded of my own weakness, and of my constant need to ask the Lord to make and keep me free from those things that would so easily pollute my life, ruin my testimony, and wreck my ministry. Beware of that Achilles heel!

One more thing on this section: a Christian is a vessel, but he is not meant to be an empty one! The old proverb does state that empty vessels make the most noise, and that is sometimes true in Christian circles. I once heard someone say that the present ecumenical debate reminded him of a public swimming pool – most of the noise came from the shallow end! That may well be true, because Christians (like others) often make a noise when they are unsure of themselves. But Christians are not to be empty vessels. Paul goes on to say that we are to 'aim at righteousness, faith, love and peace, along with those who call upon the Lord from a pure heart'. The best way to keep a vessel empty of what is polluted is to keep it full of that which is pure. A room full of light can have no darkness. The surest way for a Christian to be unpolluted is to keep on being filled with the Holy Spirit.

6. A CHRISTIAN IS A SERVANT – HE MUST NOT ASSERT HIMSELF.

'And the Lord's servant must not be quarrelsome but kindly to everyone, an apt teacher, forbearing, correcting his opponents with gentleness' (2 Timothy 2.24–25).

The word 'servant' is often used in the New Testament to describe a Christian, and some of the lessons to be drawn from this are very obvious. But as with our previous studies, let us begin with the immediate point that Paul is making in these verses. As we have already seen, Timothy was responsible for the welfare of a local fellowship of Christians, and what Paul is saying is that alongside the unflinching discipline, the firm declaration of the truth, and the fearless rooting out of false doctrine and behaviour in the church, there must also be kindness and gentleness, and the complete absence of a quarrelsome, assertive spirit.

Now let us move straight from there to the wider application of what Paul is saying. He uses the fascinating phrase 'the Lord's servant', and it *is* a fascinating one, because 'the servant of the Lord' is one of the titles used in the prophecy of Isaiah about the coming Messiah, the Lord Jesus Christ. Several sections in Isaiah between 42.1 and 53.12 are known as 'servant' passages, and in them we are told that one of the distinctive characteristics of the Messiah would be his refusal to assert himself even when persecuted and provoked. One verse speaks of this in a most moving way: 'He was oppressed and he was afflicted, yet he opened not his mouth; like a lamb that is led to the slaughter, and like a sheep that before its shearers is dumb, so he opened not his mouth' (Isaiah 53.7). What a perfect description of Christ's behaviour! As Peter puts it: 'When he was reviled, he did not revile in return; when he suffered he did not

142

threaten; but he trusted to him who judges justly' (1 Peter 2.23).

And the servant is to be like his Lord! As everywhere else in the field of behaviour, Christ left us 'an example, that you should follow in his steps' (1 Peter 2.21). The characteristic servant of the Lord is to be gentle, gracious, forgiving, courteous and understanding – and not to assert himself. Even when Paul, a little later in this Epistle, commands Timothy to 'convince, rebuke and exhort', he says that in doing so he is to be 'unfailing in patience and in teaching' (2 Timothy 4.2). Unfailing in patience! – does that set the bar higher than your own personal best? What a tragedy it is that some Christians, while having a great grasp of biblical truth, and a commendable zeal for evangelism, also display the sweet approachability of an ancient porcupine, and the tenderness of a runaway bulldozer!

But we close our series of studies not on a point of detail, but on one of principle. A Christian is 'the *Lord*'s servant', and when all the finer points of theology have been debated, when all the scholars have had their say, when all the authorities have been consulted, and when all the translations have been compared, nothing remains more simple yet demanding than that the Christian is called upon to live a life of utter obedience to all the revealed will of God, and thus reflect in his life the one who alone has the right to reign over him. It is only what a Christian is *in the world* that will account for anything in the Kingdom of God.

Some years ago, a Dr. D. J. Hiley was a Baptist minister in Bristol. His son chose the medical profession for his career, and for a while used a room in his father's house as a surgery. Late one night, there was a ring at the front doorbell. The minister threw open an upstairs window and asked what the caller wanted. 'I want Dr. Hiley, please.' 'Yes,' the minister answered, 'I am Dr. Hiley.' Back came the reply: 'But I don't want the one who preaches, I want the one who practises.'

The message, surely, is loud and clear.